School Leader Internship

Developing, Monitoring, and Evaluating Your Leadership Experience

Third Edition

Meeting Educational Leadership Policy:
ISLLC 2008, NCATE, and ELCC Standards

Gary E. Martin, Arnold B. Danzig, William F. Wright,
Richard A. Flanary, and Fred Brown

Routledge
Taylor & Francis Group
New York London

First published 2012 by Eye On Education

Published 2013 by Routledge
711 Third Avenue, New York, NY 10017, USA
2 Park Square, Milton Park, Abingdon, Oxon OX14 4RN

Routledge is an imprint of the Taylor & Francis Group, an informa business

Cover Designer: Knoll Gilbert
Cover Image: Volodymyr Goinyk | Shutterstock

Library of Congress Cataloging-in-Publication Data

Martin, Gary E., 1949 July 16–
School leader internship : developing, monitoring and evaluating your leadership experience/Gary E. Martin, Arnold B. Danzig, William F. Wright.—3rd ed.
    p.   cm.
"Meeting Educational Leadership Policy: ISLLC 2008, NCATE, and ELCC Standards"—T.p.
ISBN 978-1-59667-203-1
1. School administrators—Training of—United States.
2. School management and organization—Study and teaching (Internship)—United States.
I. Danzig, Arnold Bob, 1948–
II. Wright, William F., 1940–
III. Title.
LB1738.5.M385 2012
371.20071'5—dc23   2011035442

ISBN: 978-1-596-67203-1 (pbk)

Internship Plan and
Final Approval Page

The plan outlined in this text and other documentation is approved for meeting the requirements of the internship.

_____

Intern (Printed Name)

_____   _____

Intern Signature   Date

_____

Site Supervisor (Printed Name)

_____   _____

Site Supervisor Signature   Date

_____

University Supervisor (Printed Name)

_____   _____

University Supervisor Signature   Date

The internship is approved and meets all requirements of the University.

_____   _____

University Supervisor Signature   Date

Meet the Authors

Gary Martin is currently Professor in the Educational Leadership and Technology Department at Lamar University. He served as President of the Board (2005–06) and Executive Director (2006–10) of the National Council of Professors of Educational Administration. He also served on the National Policy Board for Educational Administration, the Educational Policy Standards: ISLLC 2008 Steering Committee, and the Board of Reviewers for the National Council for Accreditation of Teacher Education. Dr. Martin has delivered over 70 presentations at university, state, regional, national, and international conferences. He trained faculties and administrators in 47 schools or districts in Texas, California, Arizona, and Iowa in the use of problem-solving versus punitive methods and published his book on the topic. His research includes leadership skill development, natural motivation, and school reform. Gary was a high school teacher, vice-principal, and middle and alternative school principal in the Texas public school system. He also served as Assistant Director for Staff Development and previously taught at Northern Arizona University, Our Lady of the Lake University in San Antonio, and Texas A&M University in Kingsville.

Arnold Danzig is Professor in the School of Public Affairs/College of Public Programs at Arizona State University and Director of MPA/MPP programs. In 2009–2010, he served as Professor and Director of the Division of Advanced Studies in Policy, Leadership, and Curriculum and Professor in Education Leadership and Policy Studies in the Mary Lou Fulton Institute and Graduate School of Education. He has served as Associate Dean and Director of the D.E.L.T.A. Doctoral Program in Educational Leadership. His research offers a humanistic vision of leadership for schools and democratic institutions, with deep and practical commitment to the betterment of individual and institutional lives. He has authored or co-authored numerous articles on school leadership, administrator professional development, and school-to-work transitions, which appear in multiple journals including *International Studies in Educational Administration, Education Policy, Journal of Educational Administration, Educational Leadership and Administration,* and *Journal of Educational and Psychological Consultation.* He is co-editor for the 2012 and 2014 volumes of the *Review of Research in Education* published by the American Educational Research Association.

Bill Wright serves as Professor in the Research, Foundations, and Educational Leadership Department at Northern Arizona University. He previously served as superintendent of schools for over two decades. He is an author, content editor, and member of the Master Teacher Academy in Manhattan, Kansas. He is the author of *Results Oriented Teaching*, and co-author of *The Board*, which is read by administrators and school boards throughout the United States and Canada. He is co-author and content editor of *Superintendents Only*, contributing author to *VIP: Views, Ideas, & Practical Administrative Solutions* and *The In-Box: For the Educational Office Professional*, and Guest Editor of *Research Reviews and Reports*. Dr. Wright consults, speaks, and trains educational leaders both nationally and internationally. He has received awards from the North Central Accreditation, National School Board Association, and Arizona School Administrators' Superintendent of the Year.

Dick Flanary serves as Senior Director of NASSP's Leadership Programs & Services Team. He leads the design and delivery of NASSP's leadership development programs and services for prospective and practicing principals, assistant principals, and teacher leaders. Dick is an experienced trainer. He has delivered training in 47 states and eight foreign countries. He is an accomplished presenter, having delivered hundreds of presentations across the country. Dick represents NASSP with various education policy groups including the Educational Leadership Constituent Council (ELCC), the Educational Leadership Policy Standards: ISLLC 2008, the National Policy Board for Educational Administration (NPBEA), the Advanced Certification for Principals, the Executive Board for the National Council of Professors of Educational Administration (NCPEA), and the American Clearinghouse for Educational Facilities. He also serves as an adjunct professor in the College of Education at Virginia Tech University. Dick was the founding director of the Southwestern Virginia Regional Principals' Center based at Virginia Tech University in Blacksburg, Virginia. Dick worked as a middle-level principal, assistant principal, guidance counselor, and teacher in Prince William County, Virginia.

Fred Brown is the former Associate Executive Director for Membership Development and Professional Outreach for the National Association of Elementary School Principals, located in Alexandria, Virginia. In his role, Fred provided oversight for the PALS/Principal Mentoring program, PALS/Principal's Help Line, National Distinguished Principals program, as well as professional recognition programs for the NAESP Board of Directors, officers, and membership. Fred also served as NAESP's professional representative at all levels of government and private business. Fred has 43 years of experience in the field of education, 24 of which were spent as an elementary principal. Fred has been involved in both professional and community-service related associations throughout his career. He was chosen as Pennsylvania's Principal of the Year in 1985 and National Distinguished Principal by the U.S. Department of Education in 1986, and he was elected President of the NAESP for 1994–95. Fred Brown is currently a national and international consultant in administrative leadership development in Portugal, the Middle East, and various other regions.

Acknowledgements

Special thanks to the interns, principals, and superintendents who provided positive comments and helpful suggestions for the third edition of the text.

Special thanks to the following for their use, review, and recommendations:
   Nicolette Arvanitis, Principal, Round Valley High School, Covelo, CA
   Mary Aspedon, Department of Educational Administration, Southwestern Oklahoma State University, Weatherford, OK
   Bonnie Beyer, Department of Educational Administration, University of Michigan-Dearborn
   Shawn DeRose, Thomas Jefferson High School, Alexandria, VA
   Heather Duncan, Department of Educational Leadership, University of Wyoming
   Bob Heimbaugh, Special Education Director, Sheridan County School District, WY
   Michael Kelly, Educational Leadership Program, Regent University, VA
   Sonja McNeely, Department of Educational Leadership, University of Tennessee, Knoxville, TN
   Melissa Patschke, Principal, Upper Providence Elementary School, Royersford, PA
   Pam Salazar, Department of Educational Leadership, University of Nevada, Las Vegas
   Daniel Smith, Principal, Luray Middle School, VA
   Billy W. Thornton, Department of Educational Leadership, University of Nevada, Reno
   David E. Whale, Department of Educational Leadership, Central Michigan University

Special thanks to the educational technology professors Lucy (Kay) Abernathy and Diane Mason, Lamar University, for writing section 3.5—New Technologies and intern activities for 11—Learning Technology and 18—General Office Administration/Technology.

Special thanks for graciously writing the foreword for the text:
   Margaret Terry Orr, Faculty and Program Director, Bank Street College

Special thanks for researching, editing, and writing in making the first edition possible:
   Vanessa Naylon, UC-Berkeley graduate and loving stepdaughter

■ Free Downloads

Many of the tools discussed and displayed in this book are also available on the Routledge website as Adobe Acrobat files. Permission has been granted to purchasers of this book to download these tools and print them.

You can access these downloads by visiting www.routledge.com/9781596672031 and click on the Free Downloads tab.

Index of Downloads
ISLLC Self-Assessment . . . . page 2
Dispositions Assessment . . . . page 6
TELSA Self-Assessment . . . . page 9

Foreword

As policy makers renew federal policy to better support K–12 education, particularly for students and schools in the most challenging conditions, they sharply focus on the preparation of teachers and leaders. Key to their policy attention is the quality and effectiveness of field-based learning, giving priority to "clinically-rich" preparation. Such national policy attention underscores what we already know from our own research and practice: quality internships are critical to preparing school leaders who can provide vision and direction for their schools, support teachers and students effectively, and optimize organizational conditions for improved student learning.

School leadership internships are the bridge between classroom teaching and initial leadership positions. They expose candidates to the range of leadership work, enable them to observe, work with and be coached by effective leaders, and be able to apply what they learn about leadership and schools in doing leadership tasks and responsibilities. Research shows that quality internships are equal in contribution and importance to program quality in influencing graduates' leadership careers and in being able to exercise leadership practices that improve teaching, learning, and school conditions. Quality internships not only introduce candidates to the work of school leaders, but they also provide hands-on learning and, potentially, skill development in critical areas of instructional leadership and change.

Key attributes of a quality internship are giving candidates responsibilities for leading, facilitating and making decisions typical of an educational leader, and supporting candidates in gaining an educational leader's perspective for school improvement. Quality internships—that expose interns to and engage them in complex school improvement work—are difficult to create, supervise, and support. Current accountability and fiscal pressures make internship development even more challenging for on-site supervisors and program faculty. Thus, interns' supervisors and faculty, themselves, need guidance on how to create and supervise such high quality, standards-based internship experiences.

This book serves both as a guide and support to fill this need. It provides guidance on how to design school internship tasks that align to the breadth and depth of current, nationally recognized educational leadership standards. It provides step-by-step guidance for interns, their supervisors, and their faculty on how to initiate an internship and evaluate interns' work. It also incorporates essential guidance on preparing for careers in school leadership.

In this third edition, Martin, Danzig, Wright, Flanary and Brown have updated this important guide by aligning the internship to the revised ISLLC standards, and incorporating relevant, actionable internship tasks, and assessment resources for formative and summative leadership preparation. Now, more than ever, this book is critical for the over 500 leadership preparation programs nationwide and the 1000s of school districts that support leadership candidates. Most important, it provides clear direction for leadership preparation programs and their institutions on how to operationalize the kind of quality internship that research has shown is both influential and necessary for our future school leaders and, in turn, the schools they will lead. By preparing our interns well, through the guidance that this book offers, leadership preparation programs can help their graduates make a smoother transition into increasingly challenging jobs and achieve greater success in supporting their schools' improvement and effectiveness.

Margaret Terry Orr
Faculty and Program Director
Bank Street College

Note to Instructors and Supervisors

This text can be adapted to a variety of needs. It was written as a stand-alone text for a yearlong capstone internship. Depending on the nature of your institution's program, it may be used for a one-semester internship, with field experiences throughout a certification or master's program, or with a combination of experiences in various required courses and the concluding internship. The text can also be used as supplemental material. You may require students to complete all or part of the text and/or provide the student with specific university requirements in a handout format to supplement and guide the use of the text.

The text may also be used for school district administrative training and development programs. Many districts are currently seeking new leaders from their faculties and sponsoring "grow your own" or local leadership development programs. The text moves beyond typical programs of providing information about "how things are done in our district" to placing teacher-leaders in positions of leadership and observing, coaching, and developing prospective leaders.

Unique Aspects of the Text

♦ *Self, Peer, and Superior Assessments* require students to plan according to individual needs, experiences, and goals. This allows interns to focus on specific strengths and areas needing improvement.

♦ *School/District Assessments* require students to plan according to school or district needs and goals. This allows interns to serve districts as they work on increased learning, overall school improvement, and individual development.

♦ *Internship Plan* requires students to assess, analyze, prepare, and present a draft internship plan for school and/or university approval. This allows interns to take leadership roles in the development of their internships.

♦ *Projects* require interns to lead. This allows interns to utilize all the leadership skill areas, as opposed to observing and/or carrying out assigned tasks. Many preparation programs require leadership of an action research project.

♦ *38 Skill and Experience Areas* require students to learn and perform leadership skills in a variety of essential school contexts. This provides interns a wide breadth of experience.

♦ *Theory into Practice* requires students to apply learning from previous coursework. This allows interns the opportunity to reflect and form effective habits and increase learning from the field of educational research. This section is provided for review and focus, not to supplant previous instruction and study.

♦ *Interviews* require students to gather additional information and an overall perspective from leaders in various positions in the school or district. This helps interns develop a network and gain insights and additional activities in various administrative/curricular areas. Interviews are recommended at the beginning of internships.

♦ *Reflective Practice* requires students to learn the art of reflection. This allows interns to develop the necessary skill of reflection in and on practice. Stressing the importance of this skill and reviewing reflections periodically are highly recommended.

♦ *Future Professional Development* requires students to analyze and evaluate their experiences and plan for further development.

♦ *Vita and Letter of Application* require students to develop professional "accomplishments oriented" vitae and relevant letters of application. This also assists interns in gathering needed documentation for future leadership positions.

♦ *Final Report* requires students to analyze, evaluate, develop, and present concluding professional reports. This gives interns the opportunity to take leadership roles in the evaluation of their internships and demonstrate the knowledge and skills they gained from their experiences.

♦ *Use of Site Supervisors* is crucial and should be a collaborative effort with university instructors. We recommend that supervisors take an active part in assisting interns in planning, monitoring, implementing, and evaluating their internships. The role of site supervisors should be developed and communicated to both the site supervisors and the interns.

Recommendations

To adequately support interns as they seek to increase their knowledge, skills, and needed dispositions, university and/or district supervisors should consider implementing the following:

♦ Stress the importance of self-assessment and peer review in developing intern plans.

♦ Meet regularly with interns to share experiences and concerns and to assist in future planned experiences.

♦ Visit individual school sites regularly or use technology and other creative methods of observing and communicating with distance education programs.

- Establish open two-way communication and trust.
- Stress the importance of reflective journal writing.
- Provide coaching for strengths and areas needing improvement.
- Critique projects and keep the focus on actions that increase learning, develop leadership knowledge and skill, and move schools toward realization of their visions.
- Require elementary-level interns to read NAESP's *Leading Learning Communities* prior to beginning their internships.
- Require secondary-level interns to read NASSP's *Breaking Ranks II* prior to beginning their internships.
- Require middle-level interns to read NASSP'S *Breaking Ranks in the Middle* prior to beginning their internships.

The authors hope the comprehensiveness and flexibility of the text will support and assist students in "raising the bar" for their internships and meeting and exceeding the Educational Leadership Policy: ISLLC 2008, NCATE, and ELCC standards.

What's New

The third edition of this book contains the following enhancements:

- A new section on technology, including activities in #11 Learning Technology and #18 General Technology
- The addition of the ISTE National Educational Technology Standards for Administrators (NETS•A)
- A revised section on reflective practice
- An update of the generic leadership skills from 10 skills to 12 skills
- New analysis questions, changed from yes/no answers to finding the extent of adequate skill
- Updated vignettes that include the appropriate national standard
- A new dispositions self-assessment is provided in the book and online
- The Educational Policy Standards: ISLLC 2008 self-assessment is now provided online as well as in the book

Table of Contents

Meet the Authors v
Acknowledgements vii
Free Downloads. viii
Foreword ix
Note to Instructors and Supervisors. xi
What's New. xiv

Introducing School Leader Internship xix
To the Intern xix
Overview of the Internship xx
    Stage One: Assessment xx
    Stage Two: Plan xx
    Stage Three: Implementation xx
    Stage Four: Evaluation xx
Background/Recommendations for Change xxi
Purpose of the Text xxiii
Standards xxiv
    Meeting the Seventh Standard. xxv
Outline of the Text xxv
Outcomes xxvi

Stage One: Assessment 1
1.1 Vita.. 1
1.2 Self-Assessment of Educational Leadership Policy Standards: ISLLC: 2008 1
1.3 Self, Peer, Superior, and Subordinate Assessment of ISLLC Dispositions 5
1.4 Self-Assessment of the TELSA. 8
1.5 Other Assessments and Evaluations................................. 22
1.6 Position and Leadership Goals 23
1.7 School/District Assessment.. 23
1.8 Assessment Summary.. 23

Stage Two: Plan 25
2.1 Standards, Leadership Areas, and Activities.......................... 25
    Vision—Educational Leadership Policy Standards: ISLLC 2008 Standard 1 27
        1. Vision/Mission 28
        2. Strategic Plan 29
        3. Data Collection and Analysis 30
        4. Effective Communication................................. 31

5. Negotiation/Consensus Building. 32
6. Collaborative Decision Making. 33

Instruction and Learning—Educational Leadership Policy Standards:
        ISLLC 2008 Standard 2 34
7. Curriculum Analysis. 35
8. School/Program Scheduling 37
9. Supervision of Instruction/Instructional Strategies. 38
10. Learning/Motivation Theory 40
11. Learning Technology 41
12. Evaluation of Student Achievement/Testing and Measurements. 43
13. Supervision of Co-Curricular Education 44
14. Staff Development/Adult Learning. 45
15. Change Process 46
16. Student Discipline. 47
17. Student Services. 48

Management and Operations—Educational Leadership Policy Standards:
        ISLLC 2008 Standard 3 49
18. General Office Administration/Technology 50
19. School Operations/Policies 52
20. Facility and Maintenance Administration. 53
21. Student Transportation. 54
22. Food Services 55
23. Personnel Procedures 56
24. Supervision of the Budget 57

Community—Educational Leadership Policy Standards:
        ISLLC 2008 Standard 4 58
25. Community/Public Relations 59
26. Parent Involvement. 60
27. Climate That Supports Cultural Diversity 61
28. Community/Business Involvement and Partnerships 62

Ethics—Educational Leadership Policy Standards: ISLLC 2008 Standard 5 63
29. Position Goals and Requirements. 64
30. Philosophy/History of Education 65
31. Ethics. 66
32. Interpersonal Relationships. 67

Political, Social, Economic, Legal, and Cultural Contexts—Educational
        Leadership Policy Standards: ISLLC 2008 Standard 6. 68
33. School Board Policy and Procedures/State and Federal Law 69
34. Federal Programs Administration 70
35. Issue and Conflict Resolution 71
36. Current Issues Affecting Teaching and Learning 72
37. Professional Affiliations and Resources. 73
38. Professional Library 74

2.2 Meeting with Site Supervisor. 75
2.3 Performing Service Activities. 75
2.4 Conducting Local Project(s) 75
2.5 Networking. 76
2.6 Organizing a Notebook or an E-Portfolio 76
2.7 Internship/Leadership Experience Overall Plan Report. 76

Stage Three: Implementation 77
3.1 Interviewing. 77
       Interview Topics and Questions 77
3.2 Theory into Practice: Using the 12 Major Skills. 78
            1. Developing Trusting Relationships 79
            2. Leading in the Realization of the Vision 80
            3. Making Quality Decisions 81
            4. Communicating Effectively 84
            5. Resolving Conflict and Issues 86
            6. Motivating and Developing Others 88
            7. Managing Group Processes 91
            8. Supporting Others with Appropriate Leadership Style 93
            9. Using Power Ethically 95
          10. Creating and Managing a Positive Culture and Climate 97
          11. Initiating Change. 98
          12. Evaluating Student, Personnel, and Program Performance 100
                  Sample Case. 102
3.3 Reflection in Action. 106
       Defining Reflection and Reflective Practice. 106
       Reflection-in-Action and on-Action 110
       Learning Reflective Practice. 108
3.4 Enrichment and Extended Learning Activities. 109
       The Power of Vision 110
       Successful Leaders Focus on Vision, Quality, Equity, and Caring 111
       The Principal and Teacher Evaluation 112
       Cultural Bias and Standardized Tests. 114
       The Case Against High-Stakes Testing. 115
       A Management Responsibility: Supervision of Programs and Personnel. 116
       Managing School Employee Misconduct. 117
       Changing Role of Schools: Success for All Children 118
       The Power of Parent Involvement. 120
       Building Public Support. 121
       The Principal and Ethical Behavior. 122
       The Power of Perception. 123
3.5 Technology and Leadership. 124
       Technology Today and Tomorrow. 125
       What Do Prospective School Administrators Need to Know
             About Technology? 126

3.6   Journal 127
3.7   Log 128
3.8   Monitoring/Formative Evaluation 129

Stage Four: Summative Evaluation 131
4.1   Summary and Evaluation of Experience 131
4.2   Reflection on Action 131
4.3   Increased Learning and School Improvement: Results
      and Recommendations 132
4.4   Portfolio Development 132
4.5   Vita Update 132
4.6   Letter of Application 132
4.7   Future Professional Development Plan 133
4.8   Internship Report 133

Appendices 135
Appendix A.1   Sample Vita and Guidelines 135
Appendix A.2   Sample Letter of Application and Guidelines 144
Appendix A.3   Educational Leadership Policy Standards: ISLLC 2008 148
Appendix A.4   NASSP 21st Century Skills 151
Appendix A.5   NAESP Standards 153
Appendix A.6   ISTE National Educational Technology Standards
               for Administrators 154

References 157
Index 163

◼ Introducing School Leader Internship

To the Intern

This text will serve as a guide for developing, monitoring, maximizing, and evaluating your planned experience. It differs greatly from previous internships in which new leaders waited for assigned tasks or had a limited range of opportunity to grow and develop. You will be challenged in each of 12 essential skill areas and a wide variety of contexts. You will plan, perform, reflect, and form new and better leadership skill habits in

- ♦ Developing trusting relationships
- ♦ Creating, communicating, and managing a vision
- ♦ Making good decisions
- ♦ Communicating effectively
- ♦ Using appropriate leadership style
- ♦ Using power ethically
- ♦ Leading groups
- ♦ Developing and motivating others
- ♦ Resolving conflicts and issues
- ♦ Creating a positive climate and culture
- ♦ Leading change
- ♦ Conducting meaningful evaluations

You will develop, refine, improve, and incorporate these skills into your repertoire, as well as gain new knowledge and mind-sets in a vast spectrum of school contexts. Examples of the differing contexts are staff development, classroom instruction, budgets, transportation, food service, technology, and other areas that make up the 38 leadership and skill areas. You will meet and learn from a wide variety of individuals, such as the personnel director, the athletic director, the principal, the superintendent, board members, and parents and community leaders.

How challenging your experience will be is up to you. As the old adage says, "You get out of it what you put into it." You are urged to raise the bar and seek a true challenge for several very important reasons. First, you will be observed during your experience, and others will clearly see the rigor and expectations you set for yourself. Second, there may be no other time when so many other leaders will take the time to teach, counsel, and assist you in your learning, development, and practice. Most important, many people are depending on your leadership to better educate the next generation of U.S. society.

Overview of the Internship

Stage One: Assessment

- Choose the school/district site and supervisor.
- Write the vita.
- Complete the Educational Leadership Policy Standards: ISLLC 2008 assessments.
- Gather other assessments and evaluations.
- Write statements of your position and leadership goals.
- Obtain and analyze school/district assessments, improvement plans, etc.
- Analyze the vita and assessments for strengths and weaknesses, summarize the main points, and prioritize areas of focus.

Stage Two: Plan

- Choose one or more activities in each of the 38 experience areas.
- Meet with the site supervisor to reach consensus on the planned activities and plan local project(s) and various service activities.
- Decide which individuals to work with, observe, and interview, and compile a networking list of these contacts.
- Organize the notebook or e-portfolio you use to document the internship.
- Make a professional presentation of the overall plan to the site supervisor and university supervisor, if applicable.

Stage Three: Implementation

- Implement planned activities and keep documentation.
- Conduct interviews.
- Practice the 12 leadership skills.
- Reflect on practice.
- Keep a reflective journal.
- Keep a log of activities.
- Monitor progress toward mastery of state and national standards.
- Adjust intern activities throughout this stage.

Stage Four: Evaluation

- Write a brief summary or evaluation for each of the 38 skill and experience areas.
- Write a summary of reflection on practice and the 12 major skill areas.
- Compile a prioritized list of school/district improvements and recommendations.
- Develop a portfolio.

- ◆ Update the vita.
- ◆ Write a letter of application.
- ◆ Write a future professional development plan.
- ◆ Present the Final Internship Report to the site supervisor and university supervisor, if applicable.

Background/Recommendations for Change

"Criticism of the ways in which men and women are prepared for school leadership positions enjoys a long history. Perhaps the only thing more depressing than an honest appraisal of current educational administration programs is the knowledge that so little progress has been made in resolving the deeply ingrained weaknesses that have plagued training systems for so long." (Murphy, 1992, p. 79). The literature is replete with calls for reform and improvement (AASA, 1960; Kaplan, 1989; Barth, 1990; Muse and Thomas, 1991; Milstein, Bobroff, and Restine, 1991; Jacobson, 1996; Forsyth, 1998; Levine, 2004).

Advocates for administrative training reform value field experience highly, particularly the internship experience. (NAESP, 1990, p. 38). NAESP states,

> Over the years the academic tracks for the preparation of principals and superintendents have differed only slightly, if at all. In this sense, school administrator preparation programs might well be characterized as generic. Many of the administrative skills essential for success are, in fact, generic to preparation for the elementary principal, the secondary principal, and the superintendent. Such skills should be consistently taught and reinforced in administrator preparation programs. However, the day-to-day activities of each of these leaders vary significantly. It is thus equally apparent that preparation programs for elementary and middle school principals should be redesigned so as to be much more position-specific (p. 22).

NAESP also states, "The structure and contribution of clinical experiences should be studied further with the goal of providing richer practical components in programs for aspiring principals" (p. 38).

Patrick Forsyth (1998) states, "Commission reports, research, and other critiques and reform reports of the last decade have raised serious questions about conventional assumptions and practices, concurring that preparation programs for school administration must confront the issues that confront school administration." Recommendations from these sources commonly include the following:

- Key stakeholders (schools, universities, professional associations) should share responsibility for and collaborate in preparing school leaders.
- Preparation programs should balance professional knowledge with relevant administrator craft knowledge, especially in the areas of curriculum, teaching, and learning.
- The professional preparation process should be restructured to take into account how adults learn.
- Changes should be based on the recognition that clinical experiences are a vital part of administrator preparation (p. 7).

Jacobson (1996) concluded, "Conventional wisdom suggests that if you continue to do what you have always done, you can expect to get what you always got" (p. 271). Addressing criticisms and calls for reform, many leading educational organizations responded with standards for programs and practice for school leaders. These include

American Association of Colleges for Teacher Education (1988)
American Association of School Administrators, (1960, 1983, 1993, and Hoyle, English, and Steffy, 1998)
National Association of Elementary School Principals (1990, 2001, 2008)
National Association of Secondary School Principals (1985, 1995)
National Board for Professional Teaching Standards—Advanced Standards for Principals (2010)
National Commission on Excellence in Educational Administration (1987)
National Council for Accreditation for Teacher Education (1982, 1994, 2008)
National Council for Professors of Educational Administration (2000)
National Policy Board for Educational Administration (1993, 2008)
University Council for Educational Administration (1987).

The numerous standards recommended by these organizations can be distilled to the following nine characteristics of an effective internship experience:

1. Clear objectives
2. Adequate planning, supervision, and follow-up
3. Problem-centered and project-centered experiences
4. Experiences that meet individual needs and goals
5. Relevance to actual and specific job demands
6. Higher-level activities (leading, deciding, resolving, reflecting, etc.)
7. University and school district collaboration
8. Quality candidates, including more women and minorities
9. High standards that are supported nationally

Purpose of the Text

School Leader Internship: Developing, Monitoring, and Evaluating Your Leadership Experience was written to meet the general standards on the previous page and the specific Education Leadership Policy Standards: ISLLC 2008 standards to assist aspiring educational leaders in the assessment, design, implementation, and evaluation of a university or district intern leadership experience. The term *leadership experience* is appropriate and signifies a radical departure from the traditional internship and/or district training program. In using a leadership development approach, the intern assumes the leadership role. In effect, the leadership experience becomes a self-strategic plan requiring assessments, timelines, allocation of resources, benchmarks, ongoing monitoring and adjusting, evaluation, and reporting.

The internship is both a capstone of educational endeavor and a beginning experience in meeting the demands of a new position and new role in educational leadership. It is assumed that prerequisite knowledge, skill, and disposition (attitude) are at an adequate level for entry into the new leadership experience. The internship requires a high level of knowledge, skill, appropriate disposition, and effort. The experience of leadership is the goal. The intern must assume responsibility for and take the initiative to create meaningful experiences that build capacity to be effective in the internship.

Warren Bennis (1989) echoed this sentiment as "What is true for leaders is, for better or for worse, true for each of us: we are our own raw material. Only when we know what we're made of and what we want to make of it can we begin our lives—and we must do it despite an unwitting conspiracy of people and events against us." The intern becomes accountable for the breadth, depth, and rigor of the experience. True leaders welcome this responsibility and the resulting balance of authority that allows them to accomplish great things. There are virtually no documented instances of troubled schools being turned around without intervention by a powerful leader. Many other factors may contribute to such turnarounds, but leadership is the catalyst (Leithwood, et al., 2004).

The intern is responsible for assessing, designing, implementing, and evaluating an experience that accomplishes the following:

+ Meets the intern's individual needs
+ Provides an adequate breadth of experience
+ Sets high standards and expectations
+ Connects research/theory and practice
+ Provides a service to the district or school
+ Develops a global perspective
+ Incorporates assessment and reflection
+ Provides experience and evidence to gain the desired administrative position
+ Is a quality experience

In a four-year study (Martin, Wright, Perry, and Amick, 2000) on the use of the first published *Intern Manual* (Martin and Wright, 1995), both supervising administrators and interns rated the *Manual* highly for its usefulness in the nine aspects listed on page xxii.

School Leader Internship, however, is only a guide, and the final project outcome will remain the challenge and responsibility of the intern. University and/or district supervisors work collaboratively with the intern in the design, final assessment, and evaluation of the internship experience.

Standards

School Leader Internship was designed to meet the standards set by the Interstate School Leaders Licensure Consortium (ISLLC). The ISLLC was organized under the Council of Chief State School Officers and the National Policy Board of Educational Administration in part to identify and establish a set of common professional standards for school leaders. It was felt that a set of common standards would provide an avenue for improvement efforts in a variety of areas of administrative leadership. "The standards set out to improve school leadership by improving the quality of programs that prepare school leaders while establishing a level of accountability of the efforts of these programs" (Murphy, Shipman, and Pearlman, 1997).

The Educational Leadership Policy Standards: ISLLC: 2008 (CCSSO, 2008) has become the national standard and been adopted in 44 states. This is because of its quality, comprehensiveness, and acceptance by many leading school administrative organizations and accrediting agencies. The new millennium ushered in a sense of working cooperatively to better prepare school leaders (NCPEA, 2000).

The intern must be knowledgeable about the professional associations that provide guidance and resources for effective school leadership. Although supportive of the Educational Leadership Policy Standards: ISLLC: 2008 standards, each association may offer additional standards, competencies, proficiencies, and other resources to assist school leaders in a particular field. It is strongly recommended that interns become active members of the professional associations of their choice for continued and further professional development. Appendices A.3–A.6 list the standards and proficiencies for these associations.

The Educational Leadership Policy Standards: ISLLC: 2008 set high benchmarks for interns to meet. Many are standards that can be attained only following full-time administrative positions. The internship, however, will be the beginning for meeting the standards. Generally, the six standards expect aspiring administrators to

- ◆ Lead with vision
- ◆ Create a culture/climate for student and faculty growth
- ◆ Manage effectively

- ♦ Work collaboratively with the community
- ♦ Act with integrity and in an ethical manner
- ♦ Take part in and respond to the larger political, economic, social, legal, and cultural community

Educational Leadership Policy Standards: ISLLC: 2008 outlines the requisite knowledge, disposition, and performance to attain each of the six standards. Additionally, the intern must use effective habits in the planning and implementation of the internship project. Utilizing reflective practice in the monitoring and evaluation phases is also required. The intern should be cognizant of the intent to begin to master these goals and begin gathering evidence of accomplishment.

Meeting the Seventh Standard

Many universities use the National Council for the Accreditation of Teacher Education (NCATE) for accreditation. It serves as the premier organization for setting standards for leadership development programs at universities. With standards being set by many entities, a working group of the National Policy Board for Educational Administration (NPBEA) funded and worked on a consensus of the various standards. The group included representatives of the Association for Supervision and Curriculum Development (ASCD), American Association of School Administrators (AASA), National Association of Secondary School Principals (NASSP), and National Association of Elementary School Principals (NAESP). The working group became known as the Educational Leadership Constituent Council (ELCC).

The NCATE and NPBEA (which currently supports the ELCC) approved the ELCC program standards. The standards include the six Educational Leadership Policy Standards: ISLLC: 2008 standards and a new seventh standard: "A school administrator is an educational leader who promotes the success of all students by substantial, sustained, standards-based experiences in real settings that are planned and guided cooperatively by university and school district personnel for graduate credit." *School Leader Internship* meets this standard for universities as well as high standards for district leadership development programs.

Outline of the Text

Stage One covers the necessary personal and school/district assessments. These include

- ♦ Vita development and assessment
- ♦ Educational Leadership Policy Standards: ISLLC: 2008 knowledge and performance assessment
- ♦ Dispositions assessment
- ♦ School/district assessment and/or improvement plans

♦   Any additional personal assessments
♦   Leadership and position goals

Stage Two covers the development of the plan. A variety of experience areas are listed under each of the Educational Leadership Policy Standards: ISLLC: 2008 standards. "Experience Areas" include relevant skills and contexts that school leaders need to gain the knowledge and skill that will help them be successful. Suggested activities are listed for each experience area. Interns can choose from these activities or may design other activities related to the area. Interns should work in each of the 38 experience areas. They are *not* required to undertake all the suggested activities listed under each experience area. In this fashion, internship plans can be individualized while ensuring a sufficient broad base of experience and high level of expectation. The final part of this section is the design of a local district/school project.

Stage Three covers the implementation of the plan. This section addresses interviewing, putting theory into practice, reflection in and on practice, keeping a log and journal, monitoring, and formative evaluation.

Stage Four covers the evaluation and the final internship report. This includes the summative evaluation, reflection, recommendations for the school/district, and individual further professional development.

Outcomes

The intern will accomplish the following by the end of the internship experience:

♦   Conduct a self and school/district assessment.
♦   Develop a vita.
♦   Complete the design and development of a professional portfolio.
♦   Compose a letter of application.
♦   Design a three-year professional development plan.
♦   Compile a network of resources.
♦   Experience the art of reflective practice.
♦   Progress in his or her current knowledge, disposition, and skill performance.
♦   Gain a leadership experience covering a wide variety of areas.

Assessment

The first step is to develop a plan for individual improvement. It should be based on a diagnosis of your strengths and improvement needs. There are many tools available to assist you with this diagnosis. You should also incorporate feedback you've received from mentors and coaches into the development of this plan. Once your development plan is complete, you must link the realities of the internship venue to your plan. Too often, development plans aren't connected to the school improvement plan. To provide meaningful developmental experiences, your plan must align with the school improvement plan.

In this part, the intern must gather and analyze various personal and school/district documents. These include a current vita, an Educational Leadership Policy Standards: ISLLC: 2008 self-assessment, a dispositions assessment, other self-assessments and evaluations, and school/district improvement and/or strategic plans. The intern will also compile a list of available resources. The following sections further explain the needed documentation. The final section provides guidelines for analysis and reporting.

1.1 Vita

The intern should complete a draft of the vita during the assessment phase of the internship. A vita lists the facts of past education, experience, and accomplishments. It can be used for learning and planning the internship and future professional development. The vita should be reviewed to note knowledge, experience, and accomplishments in specific leadership areas as well as inexperience in other areas. The internship experience should be cited and added to the vita at the end of the internship. A sample vita and guidelines for the vita development are listed in Appendix A.1.

1.2 Self-Assessment of Educational Leadership Policy Standards: ISLLC: 2008

As of 2012, all major educational leadership professional organizations and 44 states have adopted the Educational Leadership Policy Standards:

ISLLC: 2008. The national standards include six areas that school administrators are expected to master as they lead their schools. They include

♦ developing and maintaining stewardship of the vision that is shared and supported by all stakeholders;
♦ sustaining a positive culture and successful instructional program conducive to student learning and staff professional growth;
♦ managing school operations and resources for a safe, efficient, and effective learning environment;
♦ collaborating with and responding to diverse community interests and needs;
♦ acting with integrity, fairness, and in an ethical manner; and
♦ understanding and influencing the political, social, economic, legal, and cultural context.

The following section is a self-assessment instrument for measuring knowledge and experience in each of the National Policy Standards: ISLLC 2008. The assessment is also available as a Free Download on Eye On Education's website at www.routledge.com. The intern should complete this assessment as accurately and honestly as possible. Use your results to assist in the development of your internship plan. Your choices are:

HD (high degree)   SD (some degree)   LD (low degree)   None

ISLLC Self-Assessment

Standard One:

An education leader promotes the success of every student by facilitating the development, articulation, implementation, and stewardship of a vision of learning that is shared and supported by all stakeholders.

Your degree of knowledge and experience to:

A.	Collaboratively develop and implement a shared vision and mission	HD SD LD None
B.	Collect and use data to identify goals, assess organizational effectiveness, and promote organizational learning	HD SD LD None
C.	Create and implement plans to achieve goals	HD SD LD None
D.	Promote continuous and sustainable improvement	HD SD LD None
E.	Monitor and evaluate progress and revise plans	HD SD LD None

Evidence for any area(s) marked HD: _____

_____

_____

_____

Standard Two:

An education leader promotes the success of every student by advocating, nurturing, and sustaining a school culture and instructional program conducive to student learning and staff professional growth.

Your degree of knowledge and experience to:

A. Nurture and sustain a culture of collaboration, trust, learning, and high expectations   HD SD LD None

B. Create a comprehensive, rigorous, and coherent curricular program   HD SD LD None

C. Create a personalized and motivating learning environment for students   HD SD LD None

D. Supervise instruction   HD SD LD None

E. Develop assessment and accountability systems to monitor student progress   HD SD LD None

F. Develop the instructional and leadership capacity of staff   HD SD LD None

G. Maximize time spent on quality instruction   HD SD LD None

H. Promote the use of the most effective and appropriate technologies to support teaching and learning   HD SD LD None

I. Monitor and evaluate the impact of the instructional program   HD SD LD None

Evidence for any area(s) marked HD: _____

_____

_____

_____

Standard Three:

An education leader promotes the success of every student by ensuring management of the organization, operation, and resources for a safe, efficient, and effective learning environment.

Your degree of knowledge and experience to:

A. Monitor and evaluate the management and operational systems   HD SD LD None

B. Obtain, allocate, align, and efficiently utilize human, fiscal, and technological resources   HD SD LD None

C. Promote and protect the welfare and safety of students and staff   HD SD LD None

D. Develop the capacity for distributed leadership   HD SD LD None

E. Ensure teacher and organizational time is focused to support quality instruction and student learning   HD SD LD None

Evidence for any area(s) marked HD:_____

_____

_____

_____

Standard Four:

An education leader promotes the success of every student by collaborating with faculty and community members, responding to diverse community interests and needs, and mobilizing community resources.

Your degree of knowledge and experience to:

A.	Collect and analyze data and information pertinent to the educational environment	HD SD LD None
B.	Promote understanding, appreciation, and use of the community's diverse cultural, social, and intellectual resources	HD SD LD None
C.	Build and sustain positive relationships with families and caregivers	HD SD LD None
D.	Build and sustain productive relationships with community partners	HD SD LD None

Evidence for any area(s) marked HD: _____

_____

_____

_____

Standard Five:

An education leader promotes the success of every student by acting with integrity, fairness, and in an ethical manner.

Your degree of knowledge and experience to:

A.	Ensure a system of accountability for every student's academic and social success	HD SD LD None
B.	Model principles of self-awareness, reflective practice, transparency, and ethical behavior	HD SD LD None
C.	Safeguard the values of democracy, equity, and diversity	HD SD LD None
D.	Consider and evaluate the potential moral and legal consequences of decision-making	HD SD LD None
E.	Promote social justice and ensure that individual student needs inform all aspects of schooling	HD SD LD None

Evidence for any area(s) marked HD: _____

_____

_____

_____

Standard Six:

An education leader promotes the success of every student by understanding, responding to, and influencing the political, social, economic, legal, and cultural context.

Your degree of knowledge and experience to:

A.   Advocate for children, families, and caregivers   HD SD LD None

B.   Act to influence local, district, state, and national decisions affecting   HD SD LD None
     student learning

C.   Assess, analyze, and anticipate emerging trends and initiatives in   HD SD LD None
     order to adapt leadership strategies

Evidence for any area(s) marked HD: _____

_____

_____

_____

1.3 Self, Peer, Superior, and Subordinate Assessment of ISLLC Dispositions

It's important to know yourself and know how others view you. This activity is designed to assess your dispositions in a number of areas. Some readers may be unfamiliar with the use of the term *disposition*. Disposition, in this context, describes a person's inclination to do something.

Dispositions are rooted in deeply held beliefs, values, and previous experiences. Successful leaders understand why they behave the way they do; they are aware of the beliefs and experiences that have shaped their current practice. Because successful leaders strive for a mutual understanding between themselves and those they serve, they often seek feedback from peers, superiors, and subordinates.

Make copies of the following dispositions assessment. This dispositions assessment was derived from previous 2001 ISLLC standards. The new Policy Standards do not include dispositions, but the authors believe in the importance of knowing and understanding your educational leadership dispositions. Distribute a copy to a peer and a superior. You may also choose to solicit an assessment from a subordinate, if applicable. Complete one copy of the evaluation yourself. Then compare the results of your self-assessment with the assessments made by others. Use your results to assist in the development of your internship plan. If you'd prefer to complete this assessment electronically, the assessment is also available as a Free Download on the Eye On Education website at www.routledge.com.

Dispositions Assessment

Please circle the indicator that you believe most accurately describes evidence of the following dispositions. This is not a recommendation form on the merit or expertise of the person, but an assessment of your perspective of the beliefs behind the words and/or actions of the person. Please complete this assessment as accurately and honestly as possible. There are no good or bad, right or wrong answers—just your perceptions. Thank you for your time and effort.

SE (strong evidence)   LE (limited evidence)
NS (not seen)   OE (opposing evidence)

Standard 1–Shared Vision

The intern believes in, values, and is committed to:

The educability of all	SE LE NS OE
A school vision of high standards of learning	SE LE NS OE
Continuous school improvement	SE LE NS OE
The inclusion of all members of the school community	SE LE NS OE
Ensuring that students have the knowledge, skills, and values needed to become successful adults	SE LE NS OE
A willingness to continuously examine one's own assumptions, beliefs, and practices	SE LE NS OE
Doing the work required for high levels of personal and organizational performance	SE LE NS OE

Standard 2–Culture and Program for Student and Staff Growth

The intern believes in, values, and is committed to:

Student learning as the fundamental purpose of schooling	SE LE NS OE
The proposition that all students can learn	SE LE NS OE
The variety of ways in which students can learn	SE LE NS OE
Lifelong learning for self and others	SE LE NS OE
Professional development as an integral part of school improvement	SE LE NS OE
The benefits that diversity brings to the school community	SE LE NS OE
A safe and supportive learning environment	SE LE NS OE
Preparing students to be contributing members of society	SE LE NS OE

Standard 3–Management and Operations

The intern believes in, values, and is committed to:

Making management decisions to enhance learning and teaching	SE LE NS OE
Taking risks to improve schools	SE LE NS OE
Trusting people and their judgments	SE LE NS OE
Accepting responsibility	SE LE NS OE
High-quality standards, expectations, and performances	SE LE NS OE
Involving stakeholders in management processes	SE LE NS OE
A safe environment	SE LE NS OE

Standard 4–Diversity, Family, and Community

The intern believes in, values, and is committed to:

School operating as an integral part of the community	SE LE NS OE
Collaboration and communication with families	SE LE NS OE
Involvement of families and other stakeholders in school decision-making processes	SE LE NS OE
The proposition that diversity enriches the school	SE LE NS OE
Families as partners in the education of their children	SE LE NS OE
The proposition that families have the best interests of their children in mind	SE LE NS OE
Resources of the family and community needing to be brought to bear on the education of students	SE LE NS OE
An informed public	SE LE NS OE

Standard 5–Ethics and Integrity

The intern believes in, values, and is committed to:

The ideal of the common good	SE LE NS OE
The principles of the Bill of Rights	SE LE NS OE
The right of every student to a free, quality education	SE LE NS OE
Bringing ethical principles to the decision-making process	SE LE NS OE
Subordinating one's own interest to the good of the school community	SE LE NS OE
Accepting consequences for one's principles and actions	SE LE NS OE
Using the influence of one's office constructively and productively in the service of all students and their families	SE LE NS OE
Development of a caring school community	SE LE NS OE

Standard 6–Political, Social, Economic, Legal, and Cultural Contexts

The intern believes in, values, and is committed to:

Education as a key to opportunity and social mobility	SE LE NS OE
Recognizing a variety of ideas, values, and cultures	SE LE NS OE
Importance of a continuing dialogue with other decision makers affecting education	SE LE NS OE
Actively participating in the political and policy-making context in the service of education	SE LE NS OE
Using legal systems to protect student rights and improve student opportunities	SE LE NS OE

Additional comments or elaboration on any previous items:

_____

_____

_____

_____

_____

1.4 Self-Assessment of the TELSA

The following self-assessment is very comprehensive and might ask you to assess possible development needs that you are currently are not familiar with. When this occurs, you will not be able to accurately decide whether the actions are important, the degree of difficulty, or how frequently a leader must deal with this area. Make a note of these and try to schedule a time to meet with your mentor or another experienced educational leader and solicit their advice in rating any items unfamiliar to you. In this way, greater learning will occur and you can better decide specific areas to include in your internship plan.

TELSA

Training and Educational Leader Self-Assessment: a tool for systematically determining the development needs of training and educational leaders

DIF Table		
Difficulty in performing task properly	*Importance of performing task properly*	*Frequency in performing task*
1 = EASY for me to perform	1 = of MINIMAL IMPORTANCE	D = I perform this task DAILY or more
2 = SOMEWHAT EASY for me to perform	2 = of SOME IMPORTANCE	W = I perform this task WEEKLY
3 = AVERAGE DIFFICULTY for me to perform	3 = of AVERAGE IMPORTANCE	M = I perform this task MONTHLY
4 = DIFFICULT for me to perform	4 = of ABOVE AVERAGE IMPORTANCE	Y = I perform this task YEARLY or less
5 = VERY DIFFICULT for me to perform	5 = of EXTREME IMPORTANCE	N = I have NEVER performed this task

After each of the sections I–X, calculate the score for each task. Enter figures in task score column. Example:

Task	Difficulty	Importance	Frequency	Task Score
Lead the development of vision and mission statements	1 2 3 ④ 5	1 2 3 4 ⑤	D W M Y N	13

Note that frequency is scored: D = 1   W = 2   M = 3   Y = 4   N = 5

TELSA Self-Assessment

For each of the following tasks, circle the difficulty, importance, and frequency levels. Use the DIF model above to make your selection.

I. Lead Analysis, Design, and Development of Instruction				
Task	Difficulty	Importance	Frequency	Task Score
Lead the determination of learner needs (perform needs analysis)	1 2 3 4 5	1 2 3 4 5	D W M Y N	_____
Lead the development of instructional vision and mission statements	1 2 3 4 5	1 2 3 4 5	D W M Y N	_____
Lead the development of an instructional strategic plan	1 2 3 4 5	1 2 3 4 5	D W M Y N	_____

Task	Difficulty	Importance	Frequency	Task Score
Lead the development of instructional policies and procedures	1 2 3 4 5	1 2 3 4 5	D W M Y N	_____
Lead the development of a classroom-based curriculum	1 2 3 4 5	1 2 3 4 5	D W M Y N	_____
Lead the development of a lab-based curriculum	1 2 3 4 5	1 2 3 4 5	D W M Y N	_____
Lead the development of an OJT-based curriculum	1 2 3 4 5	1 2 3 4 5	D W M Y N	_____
Lead the development of a distance learning-based curriculum	1 2 3 4 5	1 2 3 4 5	D W M Y N	_____
Lead the development of core course components: objectives, lesson plan, and tools for measuring learning and instructional effectiveness	1 2 3 4 5	1 2 3 4 5	D W M Y N	_____
Lead the selection of instructional methodologies based on learning styles	1 2 3 4 5	1 2 3 4 5	D W M Y N	_____
Lead the selection of commercially-available reading materials	1 2 3 4 5	1 2 3 4 5	D W M Y N	_____
Lead the selection of commercially-available audiovisual materials	1 2 3 4 5	1 2 3 4 5	D W M Y N	_____
Lead the selection of commercially-available instructional software	1 2 3 4 5	1 2 3 4 5	D W M Y N	_____
Lead the selection of commercially-available facility classroom, lab, and OJT materials, supplies, and equipment	1 2 3 4 5	1 2 3 4 5	D W M Y N	_____
Lead the selection of commercially-available self-paced written materials	1 2 3 4 5	1 2 3 4 5	D W M Y N	_____
Lead the selection of commercially-available case studies	1 2 3 4 5	1 2 3 4 5	D W M Y N	_____
Lead the selection of commercially-available simulations and games	1 2 3 4 5	1 2 3 4 5	D W M Y N	_____

Task	Difficulty	Importance	Frequency	Task Score
Lead the selection of commercially-available distance learning systems	1 2 3 4 5	1 2 3 4 5	D W M Y N	_____
Lead the in-house development of self-paced materials	1 2 3 4 5	1 2 3 4 5	D W M Y N	_____
Lead the in-house development of case studies	1 2 3 4 5	1 2 3 4 5	D W M Y N	_____
Lead the in-house development of simulations and games	1 2 3 4 5	1 2 3 4 5	D W M Y N	_____
Lead the in-house development of distance learning systems	1 2 3 4 5	1 2 3 4 5	D W M Y N	_____

Add all the section task scores. Enter scores on page after section X.

II. Lead Implementation of Instruction

Task	Difficulty	Importance	Frequency	Task Score
Market new instructional program to bosses	1 2 3 4 5	1 2 3 4 5	D W M Y N	_____
Market new instructional program to staff	1 2 3 4 5	1 2 3 4 5	D W M Y N	_____
Market new instructional programs to learners	1 2 3 4 5	1 2 3 4 5	D W M Y N	_____
Market new instructional program to other stakeholders (parents, line managers, customers, etc.)	1 2 3 4 5	1 2 3 4 5	D W M Y N	_____
Develop instructional calendar/schedule	1 2 3 4 5	1 2 3 4 5	D W M Y N	_____
Promote learner attendance through publicity of programs	1 2 3 4 5	1 2 3 4 5	D W M Y N	_____
Ensure the availability of instructors	1 2 3 4 5	1 2 3 4 5	D W M Y N	_____
Ensure the availability of instructional facilities	1 2 3 4 5	1 2 3 4 5	D W M Y N	_____
Ensure the availability of instructional resources	1 2 3 4 5	1 2 3 4 5	D W M Y N	_____

Task	Difficulty	Importance	Frequency	Task Score
Ensure delivery of instruction in compliance with organizational and governmental procedures, rules, and regulations	1 2 3 4 5	1 2 3 4 5	D W M Y N	_____
Motivate learners to apply themselves	1 2 3 4 5	1 2 3 4 5	D W M Y N	_____
Inspire learners to practice life-long learning	1 2 3 4 5	1 2 3 4 5	D W M Y N	_____
Maintain learner records	1 2 3 4 5	1 2 3 4 5	D W M Y N	_____
Maintain instructor records	1 2 3 4 5	1 2 3 4 5	D W M Y N	_____
Maintain program records	1 2 3 4 5	1 2 3 4 5	D W M Y N	_____

Add all the section task scores. Enter scores on page after section X.

III. Lead Evaluation of Instruction

Task	Difficulty	Importance	Frequency	Task Score
Critique instructional vision and mission statements	1 2 3 4 5	1 2 3 4 5	D W M Y N	_____
Critique an instructional strategic plan	1 2 3 4 5	1 2 3 4 5	D W M Y N	_____
Critique instructional policies and procedures	1 2 3 4 5	1 2 3 4 5	D W M Y N	_____
Critique a curriculum	1 2 3 4 5	1 2 3 4 5	D W M Y N	_____
Critique course objectives/ goals	1 2 3 4 5	1 2 3 4 5	D W M Y N	_____
Critique a lesson plan	1 2 3 4 5	1 2 3 4 5	D W M Y N	_____
Critique lesson objectives	1 2 3 4 5	1 2 3 4 5	D W M Y N	_____
Critique a multiple-choice test	1 2 3 4 5	1 2 3 4 5	D W M Y N	_____
Critique a short answer test	1 2 3 4 5	1 2 3 4 5	D W M Y N	_____
Critique an essay test	1 2 3 4 5	1 2 3 4 5	D W M Y N	_____
Critique a matching test	1 2 3 4 5	1 2 3 4 5	D W M Y N	_____
Critique a fill-in-the-blank test	1 2 3 4 5	1 2 3 4 5	D W M Y N	_____
Critique a performance-based test	1 2 3 4 5	1 2 3 4 5	D W M Y N	_____

Task	Difficulty	Importance	Frequency	Task Score
Critique performance standards/identified desired outcomes	1 2 3 4 5	1 2 3 4 5	D W M Y N	_____
Critique instructions for student projects, research papers, and assignments	1 2 3 4 5	1 2 3 4 5	D W M Y N	_____
Critique alternative assessment methods (portfolios, self-evaluation, peer evaluation, rubrics)	1 2 3 4 5	1 2 3 4 5	D W M Y N	_____
Critique lesson plan transparencies	1 2 3 4 5	1 2 3 4 5	D W M Y N	_____
Critique computerized slide show for lesson plan	1 2 3 4 5	1 2 3 4 5	D W M Y N	_____
Critique computer- based training program	1 2 3 4 5	1 2 3 4 5	D W M Y N	_____
Critique slide projector show for lesson plan	1 2 3 4 5	1 2 3 4 5	D W M Y N	_____
Critique student handouts/ guides	1 2 3 4 5	1 2 3 4 5	D W M Y N	_____
Critique classroom course package	1 2 3 4 5	1 2 3 4 5	D W M Y N	_____
Critique laboratory course package	1 2 3 4 5	1 2 3 4 5	D W M Y N	_____
Critique distance learning course package	1 2 3 4 5	1 2 3 4 5	D W M Y N	_____
Critique on-the-job-training (OJT) package	1 2 3 4 5	1 2 3 4 5	D W M Y N	_____
Critique classroom course in person	1 2 3 4 5	1 2 3 4 5	D W M Y N	_____
Critique laboratory course in person	1 2 3 4 5	1 2 3 4 5	D W M Y N	_____
Critique distance learning course in person	1 2 3 4 5	1 2 3 4 5	D W M Y N	_____
Critique on-the-job training (OJT) in person	1 2 3 4 5	1 2 3 4 5	D W M Y N	_____
Evaluate test scores to determine the effectiveness of instruction	1 2 3 4 5	1 2 3 4 5	D W M Y N	_____

Task	Difficulty	Importance	Frequency	Task Score
Evaluate learner feedback to determine the effectiveness of instruction	1 2 3 4 5	1 2 3 4 5	D W M Y N	_____
Evaluate other stakeholder (parent, management, customer, etc.) feedback to determine the effectiveness of instruction	1 2 3 4 5	1 2 3 4 5	D W M Y N	_____
Provide in-person feedback to staff after you have observed course	1 2 3 4 5	1 2 3 4 5	D W M Y N	_____
Take corrective action when instructional goals and objectives are not being met	1 2 3 4 5	1 2 3 4 5	D W M Y N	_____

Add all the section task scores. Enter scores on page after section X.

IV. Lead Staff Development

Task	Difficulty	Importance	Frequency	Task Score
Perform staff development needs analysis	1 2 3 4 5	1 2 3 4 5	D W M Y N	_____
Establish major staff development goals	1 2 3 4 5	1 2 3 4 5	D W M Y N	_____
Help staff members in writing their individual development plans	1 2 3 4 5	1 2 3 4 5	D W M Y N	_____
Help determine an activity best suited to address staff development needs (seminars, training courses, reading, coaching, etc.)	1 2 3 4 5	1 2 3 4 5	D W M Y N	_____
Monitor staff development goals and plans	1 2 3 4 5	1 2 3 4 5	D W M Y N	_____
Take corrective action when staff member is behind in meeting individual goals	1 2 3 4 5	1 2 3 4 5	D W M Y N	_____
Conduct an informal one-on-one performance appraisal session with staff member	1 2 3 4 5	1 2 3 4 5	D W M Y N	_____
Provide feedback to staff concerning progress toward development goals and objectives	1 2 3 4 5	1 2 3 4 5	D W M Y N	_____

Task	Difficulty	Importance	Frequency	Task Score
Lead a staff training session	1 2 3 4 5	1 2 3 4 5	D W M Y N	_____
Discuss learning from previous staff training session to build bridge to current session	1 2 3 4 5	1 2 3 4 5	D W M Y N	_____
Discuss anticipated learning in staff training session	1 2 3 4 5	1 2 3 4 5	D W M Y N	_____
Present subject matter in staff training session while employing effective questioning/involvement techniques	1 2 3 4 5	1 2 3 4 5	D W M Y N	_____
Demonstrate/model task during staff training session, while practicing effective questioning and involvement techniques	1 2 3 4 5	1 2 3 4 5	D W M Y N	_____
Observe staff demonstrate/ perform task during staff training session, while practicing effective questioning, involvement techniques and providing feedback	1 2 3 4 5	1 2 3 4 5	D W M Y N	_____
Provide staff with examples to assist them in application of training session concepts on the job	1 2 3 4 5	1 2 3 4 5	D W M Y N	_____
Motivate staff to master knowledge, skills, and ability during staff training session	1 2 3 4 5	1 2 3 4 5	D W M Y N	_____
Lead case study analysis during staff training session	1 2 3 4 5	1 2 3 4 5	D W M Y N	_____
Summarize learning at end of staff training session	1 2 3 4 5	1 2 3 4 5	D W M Y N	_____
Solicit post-staff training session feedback	1 2 3 4 5	1 2 3 4 5	D W M Y N	_____
Use post-staff training session feedback to improve instructional effectiveness	1 2 3 4 5	1 2 3 4 5	D W M Y N	_____
Inspire staff to practice lifelong learning	1 2 3 4 5	1 2 3 4 5	D W M Y N	_____

Add all the section task scores. Enter scores on page after section X.

V. Perform Learner-Related Administrative Duties

Task	Difficulty	Importance	Frequency	Task Score
Counsel learner about school, work	1 2 3 4 5	1 2 3 4 5	D W M Y N	_____
Counsel learner who comes to you with problems	1 2 3 4 5	1 2 3 4 5	D W M Y N	_____
Make accommodations for disabled learner in accordance with federal law	1 2 3 4 5	1 2 3 4 5	D W M Y N	_____
Deal with learner who is chronically late or absent from class	1 2 3 4 5	1 2 3 4 5	D W M Y N	_____
Deal with learner observed cheating on an examination	1 2 3 4 5	1 2 3 4 5	D W M Y N	_____
Deal with learner who is passively hostile, resistant to learning	1 2 3 4 5	1 2 3 4 5	D W M Y N	_____
Deal with learner who is functionally illiterate	1 2 3 4 5	1 2 3 4 5	D W M Y N	_____
Deal with learner who is not performing up to her/his abilities	1 2 3 4 5	1 2 3 4 5	D W M Y N	_____
Deal with learner who is angry with you	1 2 3 4 5	1 2 3 4 5	D W M Y N	_____
Deal with a learner who is feuding with another learner	1 2 3 4 5	1 2 3 4 5	D W M Y N	_____
Deal with learner who is harassing another individual	1 2 3 4 5	1 2 3 4 5	D W M Y N	_____
Deal with a learner who is verbally disrupting the learning process	1 2 3 4 5	1 2 3 4 5	D W M Y N	_____
Discipline a learner	1 2 3 4 5	1 2 3 4 5	D W M Y N	_____

Add all the section task scores. Enter scores on page after section X.

VI. Perform Staff-Related Administrative Duties

Task	Difficulty	Importance	Frequency	Task Score
Screen applications and résumés	1 2 3 4 5	1 2 3 4 5	D W M Y N	_____
Interview job applicants in compliance with the law	1 2 3 4 5	1 2 3 4 5	D W M Y N	_____
Select the most qualified candidate for a position	1 2 3 4 5	1 2 3 4 5	D W M Y N	_____
Make accommodations for disabled staff members in accordance with federal law	1 2 3 4 5	1 2 3 4 5	D W M Y N	_____
Orient staff to organizational policies and procedures; pay and benefits	1 2 3 4 5	1 2 3 4 5	D W M Y N	_____
Provide staff with on-the-job training (coach one-on-one)	1 2 3 4 5	1 2 3 4 5	D W M Y N	_____
Communicate your work performance expectations to staff	1 2 3 4 5	1 2 3 4 5	D W M Y N	_____
Manage by walking around and listening	1 2 3 4 5	1 2 3 4 5	D W M Y N	_____
Conduct staff meeting	1 2 3 4 5	1 2 3 4 5	D W M Y N	_____
Communicate bad news to your staff	1 2 3 4 5	1 2 3 4 5	D W M Y N	_____
Provide a staff member with constructive criticism of her/his work	1 2 3 4 5	1 2 3 4 5	D W M Y N	_____
Motivate your staff	1 2 3 4 5	1 2 3 4 5	D W M Y N	_____
Praise/express appreciation/reward an employee for good work	1 2 3 4 5	1 2 3 4 5	D W M Y N	_____
Conduct a formal employee performance appraisal	1 2 3 4 5	1 2 3 4 5	D W M Y N	_____
Counsel staff member who comes to you with *work* problems	1 2 3 4 5	1 2 3 4 5	D W M Y N	_____
Deal with staff member who comes to you with *personal* problems	1 2 3 4 5	1 2 3 4 5	D W M Y N	_____

Deal with staff member who is chronically late or absent from work	1 2 3 4 5	1 2 3 4 5	D W M Y N	_____
Deal with a staff member who is angry with you	1 2 3 4 5	1 2 3 4 5	D W M Y N	_____
Respond to a situation in which the quality of a staff member's work goes into a rapid decline	1 2 3 4 5	1 2 3 4 5	D W M Y N	_____
Deal with a staff member who is suspected of substance abuse	1 2 3 4 5	1 2 3 4 5	D W M Y N	_____
Deal with staff member who is harassing another individual	1 2 3 4 5	1 2 3 4 5	D W M Y N	_____
Deal with a staff member who is continually causing dissension amongst the ranks	1 2 3 4 5	1 2 3 4 5	D W M Y N	_____
Deal with feuding employees	1 2 3 4 5	1 2 3 4 5	D W M Y N	_____
Discipline a staff member	1 2 3 4 5	1 2 3 4 5	D W M Y N	_____
Lay off staff member	1 2 3 4 5	1 2 3 4 5	D W M Y N	_____
Fire staff member	1 2 3 4 5	1 2 3 4 5	D W M Y N	_____

Add all the section task scores. Enter scores on page after section X.

VII. Perform Budgetary and Other Administrative Duties

Task	Difficulty	Importance	Frequency	Task Score
Develop non-instructional plans for your organization (financial, construction, manpower, etc.)	1 2 3 4 5	1 2 3 4 5	D W M Y N	_____
Develop non-instructional goals and objectives for your organization (financial, construction, manpower, etc.)	1 2 3 4 5	1 2 3 4 5	D W M Y N	_____
Determine non-instructional material and supply requirements for your organization	1 2 3 4 5	1 2 3 4 5	D W M Y N	_____
Procure non-instructional material and supplies for your organization	1 2 3 4 5	1 2 3 4 5	D W M Y N	_____

Task	Difficulty	Importance	Frequency	Task Score
Develop a budget for your organization	1 2 3 4 5	1 2 3 4 5	D W M Y N	_____
Monitor your organization's progress in meeting non-instructional goals and objectives—report status to your boss	1 2 3 4 5	1 2 3 4 5	D W M Y N	_____
Monitor your organization's budget—report status to your boss	1 2 3 4 5	1 2 3 4 5	D W M Y N	_____
Take corrective action when your organization is behind in meeting a non-instructional goal or objective	1 2 3 4 5	1 2 3 4 5	D W M Y N	_____
Take corrective action when your organization is headed toward running over budget	1 2 3 4 5	1 2 3 4 5	D W M Y N	_____
Lead a proposal writing effort to obtain money, work	1 2 3 4 5	1 2 3 4 5	D W M Y N	_____
Inspect facility for safety problems	1 2 3 4 5	1 2 3 4 5	D W M Y N	_____
Maintain facility in good condition	1 2 3 4 5	1 2 3 4 5	D W M Y N	_____

Add all the section task scores. Enter scores on page after section X.

VIII. Communicate/Use Communication Technology

Task	Difficulty	Importance	Frequency	Task Score
Write administrative reports, papers, correspondence	1 2 3 4 5	1 2 3 4 5	D W M Y N	_____
Make a presentation	1 2 3 4 5	1 2 3 4 5	D W M Y N	_____
Communicate in person with a large group (100+ people)	1 2 3 4 5	1 2 3 4 5	D W M Y N	_____
Tell your boss bad news	1 2 3 4 5	1 2 3 4 5	D W M Y N	_____
Accept and use constructive criticism from your boss	1 2 3 4 5	1 2 3 4 5	D W M Y N	_____
Offer constructive criticism to your boss	1 2 3 4 5	1 2 3 4 5	D W M Y N	_____

Task	Difficulty	Importance	Frequency	Task Score
Tell other stakeholders (parents, managers, customers, learners, instructors, peers) bad news	1 2 3 4 5	1 2 3 4 5	D W M Y N	_____
Accept and use constructive criticism from other stakeholders (parents, managers, customers, learners, instructors, peers)	1 2 3 4 5	1 2 3 4 5	D W M Y N	_____
Operate a computer	1 2 3 4 5	1 2 3 4 5	D W M Y N	_____
Operate a printer	1 2 3 4 5	1 2 3 4 5	D W M Y N	_____
Operate a scanner	1 2 3 4 5	1 2 3 4 5	D W M Y N	_____
Use word processing software	1 2 3 4 5	1 2 3 4 5	D W M Y N	_____
Use spreadsheet software	1 2 3 4 5	1 2 3 4 5	D W M Y N	_____
Use project management software	1 2 3 4 5	1 2 3 4 5	D W M Y N	_____
Use presentation software	1 2 3 4 5	1 2 3 4 5	D W M Y N	_____
Access/use the Internet	1 2 3 4 5	1 2 3 4 5	D W M Y N	_____
Access/use organizational intranet	1 2 3 4 5	1 2 3 4 5	D W M Y N	_____
Use e-mail system	1 2 3 4 5	1 2 3 4 5	D W M Y N	_____
Operate a slide projector	1 2 3 4 5	1 2 3 4 5	D W M Y N	_____
Operate an overhead projector	1 2 3 4 5	1 2 3 4 5	D W M Y N	_____
Operate a VCR	1 2 3 4 5	1 2 3 4 5	D W M Y N	_____
Operate an LCD projector	1 2 3 4 5	1 2 3 4 5	D W M Y N	_____

Add all the section task scores. Enter scores on page after section X.

IX. Self Development

Task	Difficulty	Importance	Frequency	Task Score
Assess your own work performance	1 2 3 4 5	1 2 3 4 5	D W M Y N	_____
Manage your time—handle multiple priorities	1 2 3 4 5	1 2 3 4 5	D W M Y N	_____
Handle job stress	1 2 3 4 5	1 2 3 4 5	D W M Y N	_____
Balance work life with home life	1 2 3 4 5	1 2 3 4 5	D W M Y N	_____
Take action to address performance areas in need of improvement	1 2 3 4 5	1 2 3 4 5	D W M Y N	_____
Obtain a mentor	1 2 3 4 5	1 2 3 4 5	D W M Y N	_____
Develop your educational/ training leadership skills, knowledge, and abilities	1 2 3 4 5	1 2 3 4 5	D W M Y N	_____

Add all the section task scores. Enter scores on page after section X.

X. Crisis Management

Task	Difficulty	Importance	Frequency	Task Score
Respond to fire alarm	1 2 3 4 5	1 2 3 4 5	D W M Y N	_____
Respond to bomb threat	1 2 3 4 5	1 2 3 4 5	D W M Y N	_____
Respond to severe weather	1 2 3 4 5	1 2 3 4 5	D W M Y N	_____
Respond to illness in facility	1 2 3 4 5	1 2 3 4 5	D W M Y N	_____
Respond to injury in facility	1 2 3 4 5	1 2 3 4 5	D W M Y N	_____
Respond to an individual in the facility who becomes violent or threatens violence	1 2 3 4 5	1 2 3 4 5	D W M Y N	_____
Respond to potential blood borne pathogen release in facility	1 2 3 4 5	1 2 3 4 5	D W M Y N	_____
Respond to hazardous materials release in facility	1 2 3 4 5	1 2 3 4 5	D W M Y N	_____

Add all the section task scores. Enter scores on the next page.

Raw Scores

_____ Divide the Section I raw score by 22. Enter the mean score here: _____

_____ Divide the Section II raw score by 15. Enter the mean score here: _____

_____ Divide the Section III raw score by 34. Enter the mean score here: _____

_____ Divide the Section IV raw score by 21. Enter the mean score here: _____

_____ Divide the Section V raw score by 13. Enter the mean score here: _____

_____ Divide the Section VI raw score by 26. Enter the mean score here: _____

_____ Divide the Section VII raw score by 12. Enter the mean score here: _____

_____ Divide the Section VIII raw score by 22. Enter the mean score here: _____

_____ Divide the Section IX raw score by 7. Enter the mean score here: _____

_____ Divide the Section X raw score by 8. Enter the mean score here: _____

Use the following scale to interpret task and section scores:

Score of 3–7 Low Priority—A score of low priority indicates that additional development in these areas is not as immediate as those in the medium or high priority areas.

Score of 8–11 Medium Priority—A score of medium priority indicates that adequate time and effort planned for additional development in these areas is needed but not as immediate as those in the high priority areas.

Score of 12–15 High Priority—A score of high priority indicates that substantial time and effort planned for additional development in these areas is more immediate than those in the low or medium priority areas. The intern should consider additional readings and mentors to assist in knowledge and skill development.

Note: Individuals should continually review their needs as situations change and awareness of needs develops and changes.

1.5 Other Assessments and Evaluations

The intern will gather and review other personal evaluations and assessments that are available. These can include

- ♦ Recent annual performance evaluations
- ♦ The NASSP Leadership Skills Assessment at www.nassp.org
- ♦ NAESP assessment material at www.naesp.org
- ♦ Myers-Briggs or Keirsey Temperament at www.keirsey.com
- ♦ True Colors

♦ *Now, Discover Your Strengths,* by Marcus Buckingham and Donald O. Clifton, 2001. The book provides instructions to take the online assessment.

♦ Other relevant assessments from workshops or university courses.

The intern should summarize the findings and note major strengths in knowledge, skill, disposition, and experience, as well as weaknesses and areas needing improvement.

1.6 Position and Leadership Goals

The intern will draft a statement of position goals and a statement of leadership goals. The position goal statement is a brief description of the desired terminal position and any positions needed or desired for advancement to that position.

The leadership goal statement addresses the purpose or motivation for leading. The statement should consider the following:

♦ What educational needs underlie my motivation to lead?

♦ What personal needs underlie my motivation to lead?

♦ What do I hope to accomplish as a leader?

♦ How will my accomplishments lead to increased learning and overall school improvement?

1.7 School/District Assessment

The final assessment report must include current school/district needs. The intern should summarize and prioritize the major goals and needs for the school/district. These can be gathered from current documents, including the following:

♦ School/district improvement plans and needs assessments

♦ Strategic plans

♦ Mission statement

♦ Recent accreditation reports

♦ Action plans

♦ Other evidence of school/district needs or goals

1.8 Assessment Summary

Following the compilation and analysis of the previously gathered information, the intern will prepare a summary for the Overall Plan Report, which is given at the end of Stage Two. The summary should include highlights from the following:

- **Vita**

  Present a brief overview of the significant experiences and accomplishments in leadership, teaching, professional development, and service. The intern may use a narrative or bulleted format for the presentation.

- **Educational Leadership Policy Standards: ISLLC 2008 Self-Assessment**

  Include a list of the major areas of significant knowledge and experience, as well as the major areas of limited knowledge and experience. The intern is advised to begin collecting documentation of evidence supporting strengths and performance that meet each standard.

- **Dispositions Assessments**

  This should include a list of major areas of consensus for having *strong evidence* of the disposition and areas of consensus for *not seen* and/or *opposing evidence* for the disposition. The intern should also note dispositions that differ between the self-assessment and either peer, supervisor, or subordinate assessments.

- **Other Evaluations and/or Assessments**

  Include a brief summary of recent past annual performance evaluations, noting significant areas that relate to leadership and overall job performance. The intern should also provide summaries/highlights of other evaluative or assessment data.

- **Position Goal Statement and Leadership Goal Statement**

  Include both statements in their entirety.

- **School/District Needs Assessment**

  Include an overview of current school/district improvement plans, strategic plans, needs assessments, and/or accreditation reports. This can be presented either as a narrative or in bulleted lists, highlighting major goal and need areas. The intern should also note priorities for the upcoming school year.

Plan

Following the review of the assessment report, the intern will design the internship plan. Stage Two lists recommended or suggested activities, guidelines for service, plans for a local project, and strategies for networking.

2.1 Standards, Leadership Areas, and Activities

The following standards, leadership areas, and activities are provided to assist the intern in the design of the internship. Under each standard, leadership areas essential to meeting the standard are provided. The intern should include all 38 leadership areas in his or her plan, unless circumstances warrant omitting one or more areas. The most common circumstance is when the intern has more than adequate previous experience in an area. Omissions of any area in the intern plan should be justified and approved by the university and/or school supervisor.

Under each leadership area are a set of suggested or recommended activities and a place to plan other activities. *Interns are NOT required to do all the activities listed. However, interns should complete at least ONE activity for each leadership area.* Interns should choose activities that align with their indicated strengths and improvement areas. Remember, build on strengths and manage weaknesses. Interns should consider the school or district goals and align their efforts with these initiatives.

It is normal for the intern plan to vary in time and effort among the leadership areas. For example, the intern may spend three hours in the area of transporting students and 30 hours in scheduling to increase the personalization throughout the school or work with the budget to find additional resources to aid remedial work in literacy and numeracy. The intent of this text is to provide the needed flexibility for the intern to address his or her individual needs, provide service to the school/district, and take advantage of present opportunities.

Listed at the end of each leadership area are the following:

- ◆ Perform other related activities your supervisor approves.
- ◆ Perform service activities to the school/district your supervisor assigns.
- ◆ Perform activities that are part of a larger project.

Often, various needs and opportunities allow for activities different from those suggested in each area. Usually, the supervising administrator will provide additional activities and seek the intern's assistance with current needs of the school/district.

Many activities cite the term *school/district*. Interns may choose to gain experience in some areas at the district level. It is advisable for the intern to pencil in an X next to the activities for which he or she has a need and/or interest in gaining knowledge, skill, or improvement in a disposition. Following this, the intern should meet with the supervisor and collaborate on the final plan.

The final plan should have a significant percentage of *experiences in leading* versus observing or carrying out assigned tasks AND a focus on *increased learning*, overall *school improvement*, and *developing self and others*.

Vision

Educational Leadership Policy Standards: ISLLC 2008
Standard 1
An educational leader promotes the success of every student by facilitating the development, articulation, implementation, and stewardship of a vision of learning that is shared and supported by all stakeholders.

Correlated NASSP Skills: (1) setting instructional direction, (2) teamwork, (3) sensitivity, (5) results orientation, (6) organizational ability, (7) oral communication, (8) written communication.

Correlated NAESP Standards: (2) set high expectations and standards, (3) demand content and instruction that ensures student achievement, (5) use data as a diagnostic tool, (6) actively engage the community.

Skill and Experience Areas for Standard 1: Vision
1. Vision/mission
2. Strategic plan
3. Data collection and analysis
4. Effective communication
5. Negotiation/consensus building
6. Collaborative decision making

1. Vision/Mission

Mark an X in pencil next to the activity or activities you would like to include in your internship plan. You must choose at least one activity in this area, either one listed below or one your site or university supervisor approves. *You are not required to undertake every suggested activity for this area.*

☐ A. Analyze the school's vision/mission statement as it relates to the school's master schedule. Too often, schools have slogans, not visions. A school's master schedule is where the vision is enacted. Determine whether the vision statement is reflected in the reality of the master schedule. Provide a summary and recommendations and include in your notebook or e-portfolio. Review board policy on vision, mission, and educational goals. Evaluate the degree to which congruence exists between the district/school vision, mission, and goals. Interview district administrators, faculty, and staff and obtain their perspectives. Assess the level of agreement among parties involved and the degree of similarity between what is stated "officially" and the actual practice in the school/district. Note policies and practices not aligned with the vision. List recommendations for greater alignment with the vision and include your recommendations in your notebook or e-portfolio.

☐ B. Review and compare two different school/district vision statements. Try to obtain these from two distinct types of districts/schools (i.e., rich/poor, urban/suburban/rural, regular/charter/private, etc.). Note strengths and weaknesses of each and make recommendations for your school/district. Include your recommendations in your notebook or e-portfolio.

☐ C. Invite relevant constituents (e.g., students, parents, citizens), and lead this group to find consensus on the development of a district, school, or sub-unit vision statement. Include the final vision statement and any relevant learning from the process in your notebook or e-portfolio.

☐ D. Perform other related activities your supervisor approves and/or service activities to the school/district your supervisor assigns and/or activities that are part of a larger project.

2. Strategic Plan

Mark an X in pencil next to the activity or activities you would like to include in your internship plan. You must choose at least *one* activity in this area, either one listed below or one your site or university supervisor approves. *You are not required to undertake every suggested activity for this area.*

☐ A. Lead a project to develop a strategic plan for increasing students' literacy skills. Include relevant persons, e.g., teachers, students, curriculum leaders, reading specialists, special educators, and administrators. Infuse other necessary skill areas such as vision, data collection and analysis, communication, etc. Include a summary of the project, results, and recommendations in your notebook or e-portfolio.

☐ B. Review the strategic plan for your school/district. Note personnel involved in the plan's development, implementation, and evaluation. Investigate support and concerns from the various parties involved. Include your findings and recommendations in your notebook or e-portfolio.

☐ C. Serve on the strategic development, monitoring, or evaluation team for your school/district. This will depend on the current stage of the plan. Log your time and duties as part of the team. Cite significant learning and recommendations in your notebook or e-portfolio.

☐ D. Review, compare, and contrast strategic plans from your school/district and another school/district. Note the goals and processes used to attain the vision.

☐ E. Include your comparison and recommendations in your notebook or e-portfolio.

☐ F. Develop a strategic plan for your chosen project. Include the plan in your notebook or e-portfolio.

☐ G. Perform other related activities your supervisor approves and/or service activities to the school/district your supervisor assigns and/or activities that are part of a larger project.

Vision

3. Data Collection and Analysis

Mark an X in pencil next to the activity or activities you would like to include in your internship plan. You must choose at least one activity in this area, either one listed below or one your site or university supervisor approves. *You are not required to undertake every suggested activity for this area.*

☐ A. Review current requirements for your school under the Elementary and Secondary Education Act (ESEA), known at the time of this edition as No Child Left Behind. Review the district's collection procedures and data collected. Interview persons directly involved, for example, the curriculum director, the principal, teachers, and students. Analyze the data collected and the perspectives from each of the persons above, and compile a list of actions needed to meet ESEA guidelines.

☐ B. Review board policy and administrative regulations regarding data collection, assessment, and evaluation. Evaluate the degree to which policy and/or administrative regulations are being implemented. Write a reflective statement about ways in which the leader would seek to improve compliance in this area. If no policy/administrative regulation is in place, review other district policy/regulations in this area. Prepare a policy/administrative regulation proposal for board consideration. Include the proposed policy/regulation in your notebook or e-portfolio.

☐ C. Review the ways in which the board of education, superintendent, faculty, staff, and community relations/information department use assessment data to impact practice. Write a reflective statement about how the leader would seek to improve the use of assessment data in the school/district. Include the statement in your notebook or e-portfolio.

☐ D. Perform other related activities your supervisor approves and/or service activities to the school/district your supervisor assigns and/or activities that are part of a larger project.

4. *Effective Communication*

Mark an X in pencil next to the activity or activities you would like to include in your internship plan. You must choose at least ONE activity in this area, either one listed below or one your site or university supervisor approves. *You are not required to undertake every suggested activity for this area.*

☐ A. Review board policy and administrative regulations regarding how the school/district/will manage communications. Assess the level of compliance with policy/regulations, and write a reflective statement describing your ideas for improving communications. Include the statement in your notebook or e-portfolio.

☐ B. Write a memo to the faculty relaying information the school/district office needs to disseminate. Survey several persons who receive the memo, and obtain advice on its organization, clarity, and intent and any recommendations for improvement. Include the memo and survey results in your notebook or e-portfolio.

☐ C. Assist in conducting a faculty meeting or staff development session. Survey a random sample of the participants for strengths and areas needing improvement in your presentation. Include the results of the survey in your notebook or e-portfolio.

☐ D. Choose two effective listening techniques, such as posing probing questions, using body language, etc., and apply the techniques in a student and/or parent conference. Personally assess your effectiveness in soliciting communication from the student and/or parent(s). Include the assessment in your notebook or e-portfolio.

☐ E. Review and analyze current policy and practices that provide a "student voice." Interview students from a variety of informal groups, and assess differing perspectives on how to effectively support the right of students to be heard. Provide a summary of results and recommended action in your notebook or e-portfolio.

☐ F. Review and critique the processes the school/district uses to monitor ongoing communication between parents and the school/district and faculty. Include your critique in your notebook or e-portfolio.

☐ G. In leading your selected project, gather evaluative feedback on your ability and capacity to give information, seek information, listen, receive information, and monitor information. Include the feedback in your notebook or e-portfolio.

☐ H. Perform other related activities your supervisor approves and/or service activities to the school/district your supervisor assigns and/or activities that are part of a larger project.

5. *Negotiation/Consensus Building*

Mark an X in pencil next to the activity or activities you would like to include in your internship plan. You must choose at least ONE activity in this area, either one listed below or one your site or university supervisor approves. *You are not required to undertake every suggested activity for this area.*

☐ A. Review board policy/administrative regulations. Assess compliance with policy/regulations. Assess the leadership culture in the school/district. How frequently do leaders use a top-down style rather than collaborative leadership? Does the leadership style the school/district leaders use most often comply with official policy or administrative regulation? Write a reflective statement discussing the appropriate use of both top-down leadership and collaborative leadership. Include the statement in your notebook or e-portfolio.

☐ B. Assist in the administrative side of planning and implementing negotiations with a teacher union or representative group. Note effective practices in the planning and bargaining process. Include these practices and recommendations in your notebook or e-portfolio.

☐ C. Choose a current issue in the school/district. Use steps to resolve issues with a small group of concerned parties. Reach consensus for a plan to resolve the issue and/or a critique of areas in which resolution failed. Include the plan and critique in your notebook or e-portfolio.

☐ D. In leading your selected project, include the steps used in building consensus for your plan. Include the steps and assessment of outcomes and areas for needed improvement in your notebook or e-portfolio.

☐ E. Perform other related activities your supervisor approves and/or service activities to the school/district your supervisor assigns and/or activities that are part of a larger project.

6. Collaborative Decision Making

Mark an X in pencil next to the activity or activities you would like to include in your internship plan. You must choose at least ONE activity in this area, either one listed below or one your site or university supervisor approves. *You are not required to undertake every suggested activity for this area.*

☐ A. With permission of the superintendent or principal, observe a district cabinet, a school administrative team meeting, or another meeting at which the leader plans to use collaborative decision making. Observe the leader's behavior in outlining goals, defining problems, seeking information, providing information, clarifying and elaborating, challenging viewpoints, assessing progress, and summarizing. Include the observations and recommendations for improvement in your notebook or e-portfolio.

☐ B. For any activities in which you will lead a group, practice each group leadership task cited in the above activity (A). At the conclusion of the meeting, ask group members to complete an evaluation of your performance of each task. Include a summary of the evaluations and recommendations for improvement in your notebook or e-portfolio.

☐ C. Survey administrators, teacher leaders, and teachers to assess areas in which they believe decisions should be collaborative. Include the perceived level of interest, expertise, the need for a high-quality decision, and support for the decision. Discuss the results of the survey with the principal, and compare agreement or disagreement with the administrators' and teachers' beliefs and current practices. Include a summary and recommendations in your notebook or e-portfolio.

☐ D. Perform other related activities your supervisor approves and/or service activities to the school/district your supervisor assigns and/or activities that are part of a larger project.

Instruction and Learning

Educational Leadership Policy Standards: ISLLC 2008
Standard 2
An education leader promotes the success of every student by advocating, nurturing, and sustaining a school culture and instructional program conducive to student learning and staff professional growth.

Correlated NASSP Skills: (1) setting instructional direction, (2) teamwork, (3) sensitivity, (5) results orientation, (7) oral communication, (8) written communication, (9) development of others, (10) understanding own strengths and weaknesses.

Correlated NAESP Standards: (2) set high expectations and standards, (3) demand content and instruction that ensures student achievement, (4) create a culture of adult learning.

Skill and Experience Areas for Standard 2:
Instruction and Learning
    7. Curriculum Analysis
    8. School/Program Scheduling
    9. Supervision of Instruction/Instructional Strategies
  10. Learning/Motivation Theory
  11. Learning Technology
  12. Evaluation of Student Achievement/Testing and Measurements
  13. Supervision of Extra/Co-Curricular Education
  14. Staff Development/Adult Learning
  15. Change Process
  16. Student Discipline
  17. Student Services

7. Curriculum Analysis

Mark an X in pencil next to the activity or activities you would like to include in your internship plan. You must choose at least ONE activity in this area, either one listed below or one your site or university supervisor approves. *You are not required to undertake every suggested activity for this area.*

☐ A. Analyze and compare the curriculum with recommendations from the following: NAESP's *Leading Learning Communities* (elementary level), NASSP's *Breaking Ranks in the Middle* (middle level), NASSP's *Breaking Ranks: The Comprehensive Framework for School Improvement* (secondary). Cite areas that align with and need change to meet the recommendations from the appropriate book. Summarize findings and recommended actions, and include in your notebook or e-portfolio. (Consider this for a project that would include other relevant knowledge and skill areas.)

☐ B. Review board policy and administrative regulations regarding curriculum development, implementation, management, and evaluation. Evaluate compliance with relevant federal (ESEA) and state laws and regulations and with local board policy. Write a reflective statement outlining ways to improve supervision and management of curriculum matters, and include in your notebook or e-portfolio.

☐ C. Select one subject or course curriculum. Note the problem being addressed when it was written. Compile a list of the curriculum writers. Note who represented teachers, the subject matter, students, the learning theory, and the community/state standards. Note whether the curriculum has any weaknesses because of a lack of representation in any of these areas. Make recommendations, and include in your notebook or e-portfolio.

☐ D. Interview persons involved in the implementation of a school/district curriculum. Describe the implementation process, and note successes and concerns or problems with its implementation. Evaluate the process used and recommendations for improvements, and include in your notebook or e-portfolio.

☐ E. Actively participate, if possible, or interview a person who has experience in the textbook selection process. Include an overview of the process, the evaluative criteria used, and recommendations for improvement in your notebook or e-portfolio.

☐ F. Evaluate the text and other reading materials for one course. Include the reading level and aspects of cultural diversity or gender bias. Include an evaluation and recommendations in your notebook or e-portfolio.

☐ G. Research the processes used for curriculum evaluation in the school/district. Evaluate methods, time intervals, and the degrees of participation by teachers, students, and administrators. Include the evaluation and recommendations in your notebook or e-portfolio.

Instruction and Learning

☐ H. Go to the website of the American Psychological Association (www
.apa.org), and search for Learner-Centered Psychological Principles:
A Framework. Apply these 14 principles to understanding the strengths
and weaknesses of the instructional program in your department, school,
or district.

☐ I. Perform other related activities your supervisor approves and/or service
activities to the school/district your supervisor assigns and/or activities
that are part of a larger project.

8. School/Program Scheduling

Mark an X in pencil next to the activity or activities you would like to include in your internship plan. You must choose at least ONE activity in this area, either one listed below or one your site or university supervisor approves. *You are not required to undertake every suggested activity for this area.*

☐ A. Analyze the school/district schedule, and make recommendations for increasing efficiency and meeting student needs. Determine to what extent time variations are being utilized. Present these findings to the person responsible for scheduling to discuss their feasibility and merit. Include your analysis and recommendations and comments from the person responsible for scheduling in your notebook or e-portfolio.

☐ B. Participate in the process of student class scheduling. Include a brief overview of the process and any recommendations in your notebook or e-portfolio.

☐ C. Meet with the counselor or administrator responsible for changes in student class schedules. Discuss the number of changes, rationales for changes, and ramifications of changes. Examine ways to reduce changes and/or better meet student needs. Include a summary and recommendations in your notebook or e-portfolio.

☐ D. Observe the opening week of school/district activities, and cite the issues concerning and/or goals of such activities. Interview several teachers and/or students, and compare the issues and goals from each perspective. Note major concerns from administration, faculty, and students. Include a summary and recommendations for improvement in your notebook or e-portfolio.

☐ E. Obtain a copy of school year closing procedures. Interview several teachers and/or students, and compare issues and goals from their perspective. Note major concerns from administration, faculty, and students. Include a summary and recommendations for improvement in your notebook or e-portfolio.

☐ F. Perform other related activities your supervisor approves and/or service activities to the school/district your supervisor assigns and/or activities that are part of a larger project.

9. Supervision of Instruction/Instructional Strategies

Mark an X in pencil next to the activity or activities you would like to include in your internship plan. You must choose at least ONE activity in this area, either one listed below or one your site or university supervisor approves. *You are not required to undertake every suggested activity for this area.*

☐ A. Conduct an audit to determine the degree to which the school/district incorporates brain-based learning theory into the instructional program. Note contributions from cognitive scientists that could assist a school/district, make recommendations for implementation, and include in your notebook or e-portfolio.

☐ B. Visit the International Center for Leadership in Education (ICLE) website (www.leadered.com), and research its Rigor/Relevance Framework. Engage faculty and/or district staff in a discussion of the Rigor/Relevance Framework. Include a summary of the discussion, noting significant positions taken and perspectives elicited from the discussion, in your notebook or e-portfolio.

☐ C. With the permission of the principal and two teachers, conduct two classroom observations using the clinical supervision model: preconference, observation, analysis, and postconference. Include a summary of the observation process and recommendations for improvement in your notebook or e-portfolio.

☐ D. Following each of the classroom observations and summaries above, complete the district teacher evaluation form for the two teachers (omit names). Note the differences between a clinical model (activity B) and the district evaluation form. Include the differences, recommendations, and copies of the completed forms in your notebook or e-portfolio.

☐ E. Observe one instructional assistant. Note duties, time spent, and expertise in academic assistance to the students. Include a summary of the observation and recommendations for improvement in your notebook or e-portfolio.

☐ F. Meet with two instructional assistants and two teachers to discuss the teacher evaluation process. Compile a list of strengths, weaknesses, and recommendations for improvement. Discuss the roles of teachers and assistants in this process. Include your critique and recommendations in your notebook or e-portfolio.

☐ G. Select and administer two types of observation and evaluation instruments that are different from the official district form. Include copies of the completed forms and recommendations for alternative evaluation forms in your notebook or e-portfolio.

☐ H. Select one class to complete a student evaluation of instruction and learning. Summarize the data, and meet with a group of students to discuss the strengths and weaknesses of and recommendations for using the process. Include copies of the instrument, an overview of the student meeting, and recommendations for student input in the process in your notebook or e-portfolio.

☐ I. Interview one district-level instructional supervisor, and assess current needs, goals, and the level of service that central office instructional staff provides. Include the assessment and recommendations in your notebook or e-portfolio.

☐ J. Perform other related activities your supervisor approves and/or service activities to the school/district your supervisor assigns and/or activities that are part of a larger project.

Instruction and Learning

10. Learning/Motivation Theory

Mark an X in pencil next to the activity or activities you would like to include in your internship plan. You must choose at least ONE activity in this area, either one listed below or one your site or university supervisor approves. *You are not required to undertake every suggested activity for this area.*

☐ A. Review methods used to encourage student motivation in the classroom. Read two articles from refereed journals on motivation strategies, and discuss with selected administrators and faculty. Write a reflection on the topic and include in your notebook or e-portfolio.

☐ B. Survey a school faculty on methods used to motivate students. Survey a sample of students, soliciting methods that motivate them to perform in school. Compare and contrast the two surveys. Include the comparison and recommendations in your notebook or e-portfolio.

☐ C. Meet with a group of similar subject-area or grade-level teachers, and review the current curriculum and lesson plans. List the traditional, behavioral, cognitive, and experiential learning objectives used. Solicit methods for including more cognitive and experiential objectives in the curriculum and lesson plans. Include the list and recommendations in your notebook or e-portfolio.

☐ D. Meet with a group of teachers, and assess the amount of teaching that is at each student's challenge level (Vygotsky model, 1978). Solicit recommended methods for achieving more instruction at each student's challenge level. Include methods and recommendations in your notebook or e-portfolio.

☐ E. List all options for student participation that the school offers. These could include clubs, study groups, sports teams, and other formal and informal groups. Calculate the percentage of students who belong to one or more student groups. Meet with several students, and brainstorm reasons students choose to belong or not to belong. Seek recommendations for encouraging more students to participate. Include the list, percentages, and recommendations in your notebook or e-portfolio.

☐ F. List all examples of student recognition (honor roll, school letter jackets, most improved student awards, etc.) that the school practices. Calculate the percentage of students who receive some type of school recognition. Survey a broad spectrum of teachers, students, and parents, and elicit additional means of recognizing students. Include the list, percentages, and recommendations in your notebook or e-portfolio.

☐ G. Perform other related activities your supervisor approves and/or service activities to the school/district your supervisor assigns and/or activities that are part of a larger project.

11. *Learning Technology*

Mark an X in pencil next to the activity or activities you would like to include in your internship plan. You must choose at least ONE activity in this area, either one listed below or one your site or university supervisor approves. *You are not required to undertake every suggested activity for this area.*

☐ A. Review board policies related to the use of e-mail, interactive technologies such as Web 2.0 tools, software license agreements, Web page construction, access to the Internet, and other school/district technologies. Review the degree of compliance between policy and the technology plan, as well as the legal aspects regarding the use of various technologies. Record your findings and recommendations in your notebook or e-portfolio.

☐ B. Using school improvement data, select a particular area of curricular need. Gather information on present and future technologies used to support teaching/learning in this curriculum/subject. Make recommendations for expanded use of technology, addressing costs, training, and current and future needs of students. Write a synopsis of your findings and recommendations in your notebook or e-portfolio.

☐ C. Interview persons responsible for purchasing, supporting, or managing technologies used for instruction. Describe the process for implementing current and new technologies. Evaluate the process used, discuss concerns, and make any recommendations for improvement in your notebook or e-portfolio.

☐ D. Observe the use of technologies in the classroom, library, and/or computer lab. Discuss the strengths and weaknesses of technology use in these areas with a librarian, technology facilitator, lab supervisor, or classroom teacher and several students. Compare and contrast strengths and weaknesses students and adults cite with respect to accessibility, engagement, and other areas described in national/school/district technology plans. Provide a summary of your observations and recommendations in your notebook or e-portfolio.

☐ E. Review the International Society for Technology in Education (www.iste .org/standards/nets-for-administrators.aspx) "Essential Conditions" and standards for school administrators to effectively leverage technology for learning. Create a plan to implement the five standards. Share the plan in a blog, and solicit input from colleagues for improvement. Summarize your findings, and include in your notebook or e-portfolio.

☐ F. Review the standards for teachers (www.iste.org/standards/nets-for-teachers.aspx). Research ways the school administration could support improving teacher technology proficiencies and technology implementation within instruction. Include your recommendations in your notebook or e-portfolio.

Instruction and Learning

☐ G. Examine the standards for students (www.iste.org/standards/nets-for-students.aspx). Write a plan to support the implementation of each set of technology standards for students within instruction. Include your plan in your notebook or e-portfolio.

☐ H. Perform other related activities your supervisor approves and/or service activities to the school/district your supervisor assigns and/or activities that are part of a larger project.

12. *Evaluation of Student Achievement/Testing and Measurements*

Mark an X in pencil next to the activity or activities you would like to include in your internship plan. You must choose at least ONE activity in this area, either one listed below or one your site or university supervisor approves. *You are not required to undertake every suggested activity for this area.*

☐ A. Review board policy and assess the degree of compliance with board policy and the education plan. Discuss curriculum and assessment of student achievement with administrators and faculty. Write a reflective statement regarding ways to improve evaluation and assessment of student achievement. Include the assessment of compliance and recommendations in your notebook or e-portfolio.

☐ B. Select one subject or course curriculum. Review the distribution. of grades for the subject or course. Devise, distribute, and collect a brief needs assessment relating to strengths of and concerns about testing procedures and grading policy. Include a copy of the assessment and recommendations for improving student performance and assessment in your notebook or e-portfolio.

☐ C. Gather and analyze school/district, state, and national normed test results. Assess the current strengths and weaknesses of efforts to improve student achievement. Make recommendations to improve student performance on standardized tests. Include the assessment and recommendations in your notebook or e-portfolio.

☐ D. Organize and lead a team of teachers to study and develop a plan for improving test scores. The area chosen should be one identified as a weakness in school performance. The plan should be feasible but may require additional funds and/or a broader base of support for its implementation. Include the plan and an overview of the team process in your notebook or e-portfolio.

☐ E. Randomly select a group of students, and elicit their recommendations for improving preparation for tests. Compile and critique the student recommendations, and address the issue of student input into this process. Include the critique and recommendations for student input in your notebook or e-portfolio.

☐ F. Lead a group of common subject and/or grade-level teachers in the development and use of a six- or nine-week departmental/grade-level exam. After administering the exam, meet with the teachers and discuss the merits of this type of testing for teachers and students. Include a brief log of activities, the group process used, the results of your leadership, and recommendations for the use of this type of testing in your notebook or e-portfolio.

☐ G. Perform other related activities your supervisor approves and/or service activities to the school/district your supervisor assigns and/or activities that are part of a larger project.

Instruction and Learning

13. *Supervision of Co-Curricular Education*

Mark an X in pencil next to the activity or activities you would like to include in your internship plan. You must choose at least ONE activity in this area, either one listed below or one your site or university supervisor approves. *You are not required to undertake every suggested activity for this area.*

☐ A. Review board policy and evaluate school compliance with policy in the following areas: coaching and sponsoring assignments and the rate of pay approved by the board on an annual basis, activities in compliance with federal law (Title IV), the medical emergency plan in place and the supervision plan implemented, insurance requirements complied with, and evaluation of personnel and programs in place. Discuss co-curricular activities with administration, faculty, staff, and students. Explore the perspectives of each group, and write a reflective paper with recommendations that might improve the quality of the experience the school/district provides for students. Include the paper in your notebook or e-portfolio.

☐ B. Select an area of interest involving co-curricular activities. With the approval of the sponsor, assist in planning and supervising the activity. Include a critique of the learning experience for the students involved in your notebook or e-portfolio. The critique should also address student motivation, discipline, and performance and the activity's relation to overall student education. Collaboratively work with one teacher in planning and supervising a co-curricular activity. Include a critique of the learning experience, using the indicators listed in activity A, in your notebook or e-portfolio.

☐ C. Meet with a group of randomly selected students to discuss the strengths and weaknesses of co-curricular activities. List recommendations for improving and/or expanding the strengths of such activities into other subject areas, and include the list in your notebook or e-portfolio.

☐ D. Perform other related activities your supervisor approves and/or service activities to the school/district your supervisor assigns and/or activities that are part of a larger project.

14. *Staff Development/Adult Learning*

Mark an X in pencil next to the activity or activities you would like to include in your internship plan. You must choose at least ONE activity in this area, either one listed below or one your site or university supervisor approves. *You are not required to undertake every suggested activity for this area.*

A. List and analyze all policies and current practices by leaders that support student development. Interview administrators and faculty, and assess the perceived effectiveness of current practices. Seek recommendations for greater efforts and better results in developing others. Provide a summary of concerns and recommendations in your notebook or e-portfolio.

B. Gather, from written evidence or from someone responsible for staff development, the yearly school/district staff development plan. Analyze the plan with respect to school mission, student achievement, and teacher evaluations. Include a copy or an overview of the plan and its relationship to the above variables in your notebook or e-portfolio.

C. Collaborate with an experienced staff developer in one staff development activity. It should include planning, implementing, instructing, and evaluating. Include a copy of the agenda, relevant materials, and the evaluation in your notebook or e-portfolio.

D. List all professional development activities completed by the faculty of a particular school. This should include activities provided by the school/ district and outside the school/district. Note discrepancies between the amount of professional development and the experience and subject areas of the teachers. Make recommendations for greater involvement in professional development by all faculty members. Include the list, patterns, and recommendations in your notebook or e-portfolio.

E. Survey a broad spectrum of teachers to elicit recommendations for more effective and relevant professional development, and assess the degree of importance that professional development should have in teacher evaluation. Include the survey results and recommendations for effective professional development and its use in teacher evaluation in your notebook or e-portfolio.

F. Survey a broad spectrum of students to discover their beliefs about necessary areas of training for their teachers. Discuss the students' responses with the faculty and/or staff developers. Compare and contrast the perceived needs from the students with the current school/district staff development plan. Include the survey results, comparisons, and recommendations in your notebook or e-portfolio.

G. Perform other related activities your supervisor approves and/or service activities to the school/district your supervisor assigns and/or activities that are part of a larger project.

15. *Change Process*

Mark an X in pencil next to the activity or activities you would like to include in your internship plan. You must choose at least ONE activity in this area, either one listed below or one your site or university supervisor approves. *You are not required to undertake every suggested activity for this area.*

☐ A. Review board policy regarding innovations and change in the school/district. Select two or three readings from respected journals, and discuss their content with faculty and administration. Assess the degree to which change theory is used to facilitate innovation and changes in school/district programs and operations. Write a reflective statement on the topic, and include it in your notebook or e-portfolio.

☐ B. Meet with a current leader involved in implementing a school/district change. Find out why the change was made and what steps were taken to make the change. Following this, survey several persons the change affected, and assess the support or nonsupport for the change. Analyze reasons that some do not support the change and recommend a way to help them move to the next stage of change. Summarize and include in your notebook or e-portfolio.

☐ C. In your selected local project, devise a plan for any change affecting other individuals. Choose two of these individuals, and discuss how they internalized or resisted the change. Include findings and recommendations with your project summary.

☐ D. Perform other related activities your supervisor approves and/or service activities to the school/district your supervisor assigns and/or activities that are part of a larger project.

16. Student Discipline

Mark an X in pencil next to the activity or activities you would like to include in your internship plan. You must choose at least ONE activity in this area, either one listed below or one your site or university supervisor approves. *You are not required to undertake every suggested activity for this area.*

☐ A. Review board policy and school handbooks. Review current practice in the school/district. Meet and discuss discipline with administrators in charge of student discipline, faculty, staff, students, and selected parents. Assess school/district compliance with law (state and federal), policy, and regulations. Write a reflective statement on student discipline and include in your notebook or e-portfolio.

☐ B. Examine the school/district discipline policy and analyze its strengths and weaknesses. Include the analysis and recommendations in your notebook or e-portfolio.

☐ C. Review discipline referrals for a specific period, and compile the data with regard to grade level, special education classification, race, and gender. Include a summary of your findings and recommendations for improvement in your notebook or e-portfolio.

☐ D. With the permission of the administration, participate in a conference dealing with student discipline. Critique the session with regard to consequences imposed and the need for additional assistance with improving students' social skills. Include the critique and recommendations in your notebook or e-portfolio.

☐ E. Meet with a representative group of selected students to discuss school rules and discipline procedures. Include an analysis of your findings and any student recommendations in your notebook or e-portfolio.

☐ F. Interview one administrator, one student, and a local law enforcement officer knowledgeable about current gang activity. Complete and include in your notebook or e-portfolio analyses of these meetings with regard to current policy and efforts to mitigate the effects gangs have on schools.

☐ G. Perform other related activities your supervisor approves and/or service activities to the school/district your supervisor assigns and/or activities that are part of a larger project.

Instruction and Learning

17. *Student Services*

Mark an X in pencil next to the activity or activities you would like to include in your internship plan. You must choose at least ONE activity in this area, either one listed below or one your site or university supervisor approves. *You are not required to undertake every suggested activity for this area.*

☐ A. Review board policy regarding student services. Assess degree of compliance with policy and education plan. Identify ways to improve student services and include in your notebook or e-portfolio.

☐ B. Participate in a career or educational program session with a counselor and a student. Include a critique of the session in your notebook or e-portfolio.

☐ C. Interview a school nurse, and discuss the major requirements, concerns about, and goals for the school health program. Address issues such as abuse, HIV/AIDS, sex education, and any other current issues. Include a summary and recommendations in your notebook or e-portfolio.

☐ D. Meet with a counselor, a member of the faculty or administration, and a parent to discuss the role of the school regarding children's response to their parents' divorce, single parents' needs, and after-school care. Include a list of concerns and recommendations for dealing with these issues in your notebook or e-portfolio.

☐ E. Review policies related to dealing with bullying directed at lesbian, gay, bisexual, and transgender (LGBT) students. Determine whether the school/district complies with policies, and assess whether practices within policies are effective in meeting students' needs. Include a summary and recommendations in your notebook or e-portfolio.

☐ F. Perform other related activities your supervisor approves and/or service activities to the school/district your supervisor assigns and/or activities that are part of a larger project.

Management and Operations

Educational Leadership Policy Standards: ISLLC 2008
Standard 3
An education leader promotes the success of every student by managing an organization, its operations, and its resources to ensure a safe, efficient, and effective learning environment.

Correlated NASSP Skills: (1) setting instructional direction, (2) teamwork, (4) judgment, (5) results orientation, (6) organizational ability

Correlated NAESP Standards: (1) balance management and leadership roles, (3) demand content and instruction that ensures student achievement, (4) create a culture of adult learning

Skill and Experience Areas for Standard 3: Management and Operations
18. General Office Administration
19. School Operations/Policies
20. Facility and Maintenance Administration/Safety and Security
21. Student Transportation
22. Food Services
23. Personnel Procedures
24. Supervision of the Budget

18. *General Office Administration/Technology*

Mark an X in pencil next to the activity or activities you would like to include in your internship plan. You must choose at least ONE activity in this area, either one listed below or one your site or university supervisor approves. *You are not required to undertake every suggested activity for this area.*

☐ A. Examine the Technology Standards for School Administrators (www.iste .org/standards/nets-for-administrators.aspx) Systemic Improvement Standard. Assess whether the effective use of information and technology resources could improve your school/district. Devise an action plan to better meet the standard and include in your notebook or e-portfolio.

☐ B. Review the job descriptions and evaluation forms for the key office personnel at the school/district (for example, administrative assistant, attendance officer). Following your review, meet with these persons (individually or as a group) to discuss their major duties, technology skills and applications, concerns, and recommendations regarding the work required and its relation to the job description and evaluation form. Include in your notebook or e-portfolio.

☐ C. Observe an office administrative assistant for a period of time to assess the needs and demands of the position, including access to and use of technology resources. Following the observation, and with guidance from the administrative assistant and administration, take responsibility for some administrative duties for a set period. Include a summary of the needs and demands of the position and recommendations for enhancing job performance in your notebook or e-portfolio.

☐ D. Inventory the current administrative technology in use, which should include phone systems, copy machines, fax equipment, security systems, computers, printers, and any other forms of technology used for administration of the school/district. Include the major uses of and any major concerns about these forms of technology. Then, review the National Education Technology Plan essential areas (www.ed.gov/sites/default/ files/netp2010.pdf) and the school/district technology plan. Assess whether the technologies currently in use align with the national/ school/district goals for implementation. Make recommendations for improvement and include in your notebook or e-portfolio.

☐ E. Review the policy and budget for administrative technology. Develop a plan to fund and implement recommended technology upgrades and/or emerging technologies to meet the needs of the administrative staff. Share the plan with the principal and include in your notebook or e-portfolio.

☐ F. Examine the school/district/classroom websites and school/district policies for updating and maintaining accurate content. Make recommendations for improvement to support ongoing school management and operations and include in your notebook or e-portfolio.

☐ G. Perform other related activities your supervisor approves and/or service activities to the school/district your supervisor assigns and/or activities that are part of a larger project.

Management and Operations

19. School Operations/Policies

Mark an X in pencil next to the activity or activities you would like to include in your internship plan. You must choose at least ONE activity in this area, either one listed below or one your site or university supervisor approves. *You are not required to undertake every suggested activity for this area.*

☐ A. Review the policies for school/district operations. Evaluate the extent to which the school/district complies with these policies, and make recommendations for increasing compliance. Include the evaluation and recommendations in your notebook or e-portfolio.

☐ B. Meet with the school/district attendance officer. Discuss the rules, procedures, and ramifications of attendance on law, finance, and general school/district operations. Include the highlights and/or a summary of the meeting in your notebook or e-portfolio.

☐ C. Review school/district procedures for opening and closing the school year. Observe or take an active part in these procedures. Critique the effectiveness of and major concerns about these procedures. Include the critique in your notebook or e-portfolio.

☐ D. Perform other related activities your supervisor approves and/or service activities to the school/district your supervisor assigns and/or activities that are part of a larger project.

20. *Facility and Maintenance Administration*

Mark an X in pencil next to the activity or activities you would like to include in your internship plan. You must choose at least ONE activity in this area, either one listed below or one your site or university supervisor approves. *You are not required to undertake every suggested activity for this area.*

☐ A. Examine reports from current local health and fire inspections and any other required state or federal reporting data on facility maintenance. Examine building work orders and work accomplished for the school/district. Include a summary of your findings and recommendations in your notebook or e-portfolio.

☐ B. Meet with the director of maintenance and/or head custodian and review job responsibilities and staff schedules. Shadow/observe one custodian and/or maintenance person for a period of time (at least one hour—more if possible). Include a brief report of the meeting and your observations, including the staff person's needs and concerns, and an overall assessment of work performed, in your notebook or e-portfolio.

☐ C. Perform other related activities your supervisor approves and/or service activities to the school/district your supervisor assigns and/or activities that are part of a larger project.

Management and Operations

21. *Student Transportation*

Mark an X in pencil next to the activity or activities you would like to include in your internship plan. You must choose at least ONE activity in this area, either one listed below or one your site or university supervisor approves. *You are not required to undertake every suggested activity for this area.*

☐ A. Interview the director of transportation, and discuss current issues and needs regarding transportation. These should include costs, maintenance, personnel issues, training and safety, and student problems. Include a brief summary of needs and issues in your notebook or e-portfolio.

☐ B. With the permission of the director, observe one bus driver during a morning or an afternoon bus run. Include a summary of your observations and any recommendations in your notebook or e-portfolio.

☐ C. Review the policies for student transportation. Evaluate the extent to which the school/district is in compliance. Be sure to consider home to school, school to home, and co-curricular procedures. Include a brief summary of your findings and recommendations in your notebook or e-portfolio.

☐ D. Review incidents and discipline problems occurring on the buses. Interview several students and bus drivers about their concerns and recommendations for making bus service safer and more efficient. Include a brief summary of your findings and recommendations in your notebook or e-portfolio.

☐ E. Perform other related activities your supervisor approves and/or service activities to the school/district your supervisor assigns and/or activities that are part of a larger project.

22. *Food Services*

Mark an X in pencil next to the activity or activities you would like to include in your internship plan. You must choose at least ONE activity in this area, either one listed below or one your site or university supervisor approves. *You are not required to undertake every suggested activity for this area.*

☐ A. Interview the school/district food service manager and discuss the current requirements of, concerns about, and issues regarding the program. Include a summary of the interview in your notebook or e-portfolio.

☐ B. Observe a food service worker in the preparation and delivery of either a breakfast or lunch meal. Include a summary of your observations, focusing on the needs and concerns of the worker, and an overall assessment of work performed in your notebook or e-portfolio.

☐ C. Perform other related activities your supervisor approves and/or service activities to the school/district your supervisor assigns and/or activities that are part of a larger project.

Management and Operations

23. *Personnel Procedures*

Mark an X in pencil next to the activity or activities you would like to include in your internship plan. You must choose at least ONE activity in this area, either one listed below or one your site or university supervisor approves. *You are not required to undertake every suggested activity for this area.*

☐ A. Interview the person responsible for district personnel. Major requirements and issues to discuss should include planning, recruitment, selection, induction, compensation, and evaluation and dismissal of personnel. Include a summary of the interview in your notebook or e-portfolio.

☐ B. With the permission of the administration, participate in an interview for a professional position. Write a critique of the interview process and include in your notebook or e-portfolio.

☐ C. Gather information from two or more administrators on relevant and legal questioning/assessment strategies used in interviewing. Compile a list of questions to use in hiring professional staff and administrators and include in your notebook or e-portfolio.

☐ D. Meet with persons responsible for personnel and discuss the factors they consider important when planning professional development, such as the experience of current staff, current evaluations, future needs, etc. Include your assessment and recommendations in your notebook or e-portfolio.

☐ E. Meet with administrators at the school/district level, and gather information on staff turnover and reasons for leaving. Gather any additional information from exit interviews. Assess the turnover rate, actions taken to address concerns, and any additional recommendations for improvement. Include your assessment and recommendations in your notebook or e-portfolio.

☐ F. Meet with administrators at the school/district level, and gather information on placement and promotion policy and procedures. Discuss the number of teachers teaching outside their certification areas and the extent to which the school/district promotes and develops from within. Include a summary of major goals, concerns, and recommendations in your notebook or e-portfolio.

☐ G. Perform other related activities your supervisor approves and/or service activities to the school/district your supervisor assigns and/or activities that are part of a larger project.

24. *Supervision of the Budget*

Mark an X in pencil next to the activity or activities you would like to include in your internship plan. You must choose at least ONE activity in this area, either one listed below or one your site or university supervisor approves. *You are not required to undertake every suggested activity for this area.*

☐ A. Examine the school budget and the various accounts under the discretion and responsibility of the principal. Analyze the extent to which funds are directly related to increasing learning. Include a brief analysis of major responsibilities, plans, reports, and major concerns in your notebook or e-portfolio.

☐ B. Interview the administrator responsible for the district finance/budget office. The interview should focus on administrative responsibility, guidelines, training programs, and any major needs or concerns. Include an overview of the interview in your notebook or e-portfolio.

☐ C. Participate in the budget planning process for the school/district. Include an overview of the process and any recommendations in your notebook or e-portfolio.

☐ D. Complete a requisition for a service or supply item from a budgeted account. Include a copy of the requisition and a brief description of the path it follows for approval in your notebook or e-portfolio.

☐ E. Perform other related activities your supervisor approves and/or service activities to the school/district your supervisor assigns and/or activities that are part of a larger project.

Community

Educational Leadership Policy Standards: ISLLC 2008
Standard 4
An education leader promotes the success of every student by collaborating with faculty and community members, responding to diverse community interests and needs, and mobilizing community resources.

Correlated NASSP Skills: (2) teamwork, (3) sensitivity, (6) organizational ability, (7) oral communication, (8) written communication

Correlated NAESP Standards: (6) actively engage the community

Skill and Experience Areas for Standard 4: Community
25. Community/Public Relations
26. Parent Involvement
27. Climate That Supports Cultural Diversity
28. Community/Business Involvement and Partnerships

25. Community/Public Relations

Mark an X in pencil next to the activity or activities you would like to include in your internship plan. You must choose at least ONE activity in this area, either one listed below or one your site or university supervisor approves. *You are not required to undertake every suggested activity for this area.*

☐ A. Interview one or more persons involved in school/district public relations. The interview should include eliciting strategies for effective communication to and from the community and the issue of community politics. Include a summary of the interview in your notebook or e-portfolio.

☐ B. With the person from activity A or someone else in the department, assist in the preparation of a written communication addressed to the community. Include a copy of the document in your notebook or e-portfolio.

☐ C. Ask knowledgeable persons in the district to identify influential groups and individuals in the community. Through brief phone interviews, discuss their assessments of communication with the school/district, issues and concerns, and recommendations for improved relations. Include a summary and recommendations in your notebook or e-portfolio.

☐ D. Using the summary and recommendations for activity C, meet with one board member or school/district administrator and compare perspectives and plans for improved community relations. Include a summary and recommendations in your notebook or e-portfolio.

☐ E. Perform other related activities your supervisor approves and/or service activities to the school/district your supervisor assigns and/or activities that are part of a larger project.

Community

26. *Parent Involvement*

Mark an X in pencil next to the activity or activities you would like to include in your internship plan. You must choose at least ONE activity in this area, either one listed below or one your site or university supervisor approves. *You are not required to undertake every suggested activity for this area.*

☐ A. Develop a general questionnaire addressing school policy, instruction, homework, activities, discipline, and parent involvement. Distribute the questionnaire to a group of parents. Include a summary of your findings concerning parental attitudes about school in your notebook or e-portfolio.

☐ B. Examine the current policy and procedures for parent involvement in the school/district, in particular, a plan for involving hard-to-reach parents. Include a brief summary of school/district initiatives in parent involvement in your notebook or e-portfolio.

☐ C. Write a short proposal for increasing or improving parent involvement with and attitudes toward the school. Include the proposal in your notebook or e-portfolio.

☐ D. Observe a meeting of the Site-Based Council. Assess the role parents play in the council's work, and provide recommendations for increasing parents' effectiveness. Include the agenda, outcomes of the meeting, and recommendations in your notebook or e-portfolio.

☐ E. Perform other related activities your supervisor approves and/or service activities to the school/district your supervisor assigns and/or activities that are part of a larger project.

27. *Climate That Supports Cultural Diversity*

Mark an X in pencil next to the activity or activities you would like to include in your internship plan. You must choose at least ONE activity in this area, either one listed below or one your site or university supervisor approves. *You are not required to undertake every suggested activity for this area.*

⬚ A. Examine and evaluate school library resources that address the heritage and values of culturally diverse populations. Include a copy of the evaluation and recommendations in your notebook or e-portfolio.

⬚ B. Meet with members of the language arts and/or reading departments, and examine the literature used with regard to gender stereotyping. Include your analysis and recommendations in your notebook or e-portfolio.

⬚ C. Develop and implement a plan to promote cultural diversity in the district, school, or classroom. Include a copy of the plan in your notebook or e-portfolio.

⬚ D. Meet confidentially with one or more students from different racial groups to assess their concerns and recommendations for creating a positive climate that supports cultural diversity in the school/district. Include a summary and critique of the interview in your notebook or e-portfolio.

⬚ E. Meet confidentially with one or more parents from different racial groups to assess their concerns and recommendations for creating a positive climate that supports cultural diversity in the school/district. Include a summary and critique of the interview in your notebook or e-portfolio.

⬚ F. Perform other related activities your supervisor approves and/or service activities to the school/district your supervisor assigns and/or activities that are part of a larger project.

Community

28. *Community/Business Involvement and Partnerships*

Mark an X in pencil next to the activity or activities you would like to include in your internship plan. You must choose at least ONE activity in this area, either one listed below or one your site or university supervisor approves. *You are not required to undertake every suggested activity for this area.*

☐ A. Compile a list of social agencies that are available to help and support students, faculty, and administration. Include the list of agencies and the major services they provide in your notebook or e-portfolio.

☐ B. Interview one social service worker (identified in activity A) who assists students or faculty. The interview should focus on the needs of the clients served and the worker's view of the role of the school in meeting these needs. Include a summary of the interview and recommendations for improvement in your notebook or e-portfolio.

☐ C. Interview two community leaders who reside in the school/district attendance zone. Focus on their perceptions of the quality of education, concerns, and recommendations for the school/district. Include a summary of the interview in your notebook or e-portfolio.

☐ D. Gather information on the resources available to the schools from the community and businesses. Analyze the extent of utilization, make recommendations for improved cooperation and mutual benefit, and include these in your notebook or e-portfolio.

☐ E. Perform other related activities your supervisor approves and/or service activities to the school/district your supervisor assigns and/or activities that are part of a larger project.

Ethics

Educational Leadership Policy Standards: ISLLC 2008
Standard 5
An education leader promotes the success of every student by acting with integrity and fairness and in an ethical manner.

Correlated NASSP Skills: (2) teamwork, (3) sensitivity, (4) judgment, (6) organizational ability

Correlated NAESP Standards: (1) balance management and leadership roles, (2) set high expectations and standards

Skill and Experience Areas for Standard 5: Ethics
29. Position Goals and Requirements
30. Philosophy/History of Education
31. Ethics
32. Interpersonal Relationships

29. *Position Goals and Requirements*

Mark an X in pencil next to the activity or activities you would like to include in your internship plan. You must choose at least ONE activity in this area, either one listed below or one your site or university supervisor approves. *You are not required to undertake every suggested activity for this area.*

☐ A. Obtain a copy of the job description and evaluation instrument used for the principal. Analyze the correlation between the requirements listed in the job description and the performance standards of the evaluation. Include copies of the job description and evaluation and your analysis in your notebook or e-portfolio.

☐ B. Review the above materials and interview one supervisor responsible for evaluating the principal. Determine the degree of subjectivity in the evaluation process and any additional criteria used that is not in the job description. Include a summary of the interview in your notebook or e-portfolio.

☐ C. Gather and compile a list of current demands/goals that the principal is responsible for. These may come from state or board mandates, the strategic plan, the campus improvement plan, or community concerns. Relate these goals to areas on the job description and evaluation. Include the list of demands/goals and their relation to the job description and evaluation in your notebook or e-portfolio.

☐ D. Perform other related activities your supervisor approves and/or service activities to the school/district your supervisor assigns and/or activities that are part of a larger project.

30. Philosophy/History of Education

Mark an X in pencil next to the activity or activities you would like to include in your internship plan. You must choose at least ONE activity in this area, either one listed below or one your site or university supervisor approves. *You are not required to undertake every suggested activity for this area.*

☐ A. Find a retired educator or an elderly community member and conduct an interview. Focus on the oral history of the community and the school system. Note significant events that affect the school/district today. Include highlights of the interview in your notebook or e-portfolio.

☐ B. Write a story about the person you met in activity A. Include biography, education, and his or her philosophy of practice. How do these connect?

☐ C. Review past school board agendas, reports, and/or minutes. Note significant events, policy changes, and recurring themes or concerns that impact the school/district today. Include a summary in your notebook or e-portfolio.

☐ D. Review the officially adopted curriculum in one area. Note the philosophical base that underlies the curriculum. Cite any recommendations for including other philosophies that would better serve the needs of all students. Include your recommendations in your notebook or e-portfolio.

☐ E. In a planned project that you lead, cite any relevant historical background. List one or more significant educational philosophers who would support the project goal. Include this information in the background section of the project report.

☐ F. Perform other related activities your supervisor approves and/or service activities to the school/district your supervisor assigns and/or activities that are part of a larger project.

Ethics

31. Ethics

Mark an X in pencil next to the activity or activities you would like to include in your internship plan. You must choose at least ONE activity in this area, either one listed below or one your site or university supervisor approves. *You are not required to undertake every suggested activity for this area.*

☐ A. Draft a list of the guiding principles for ethical behavior that you currently employ. Interview one school and one business/civic leader, and ask about the principles they employ. Compare and contrast the lists and determine whether there is any impact on increased learning and school improvement. Include the lists, comparisons, and recommendations in your notebook or e-portfolio.

☐ B. Meet with a group of school staff members, for example, administrative assistants, clerks, etc., and discuss their perspectives of ethical/unethical behaviors of certified personnel in the school/district. Seek recommendations for policy changes, additional training, and/or consequences to ensure that the practices of certified personnel are ethical. Include the recommendations in your notebook or e-portfolio.

☐ C. Meet with a representative group of students. Solicit their beliefs about and experiences with ethical practices in the school or classroom. Using the students' perspectives, make recommendations for ensuring the ethical behavior of all students and include in your notebook or e-portfolio.

☐ D. Following the completion of your local project, consider the ethical beliefs that guided each of your actions. Discuss these beliefs with others involved in the project. Include feedback and any recommendations in your notebook or e-portfolio.

☐ E. Provide evidence for demonstrating that you actually *do* what you tell others to do. For example, if you ask others to monitor and adjust their performances, show how you do this in your work. Include evidence in your notebook or e-portfolio.

☐ F. Perform other related activities your supervisor approves and/or service activities to the school/district your supervisor assigns and/or activities that are part of a larger project.

32. *Interpersonal Relationships*

Mark an X in pencil next to the activity or activities you would like to include in your internship plan. You must choose at least ONE activity in this area, either one listed below or one your site or university supervisor approves. *You are not required to undertake every suggested activity for this area.*

☐ A. Choose from the following list of interpersonal skills the ones you wish to develop throughout the school year. It is recommended that you choose two to four, but you may add others as you become proficient in your first choices.

- Converses with others in a positive and pleasant manner
- Avoids criticizing and values diverse opinions/perspectives
- Avoids interrupting others who are speaking
- Acknowledges accomplishments of others
- Promptly responds to others with concerns or needs
- Shares information with others that need to know
- Accepts criticism
- Avoids being defensive when challenged
- Shares self with others
- Seeks to know and understand others

When leading meetings,

- Encourages others to participate
- Acknowledges feelings and mood relationships within the group
- Eases tensions when they occur
- Attempts to resolve conflicts constructively
- Encourages consideration of varying perspectives
- Is empathetic with others
- Shares responsibilities

☐ B. Perform other related activities your supervisor approves and/or service activities to the school/district your supervisor assigns and/or activities that are part of a larger project.

Ethics

Political, Social, Legal, Economic, and Cultural Context

Educational Leadership Policy Standards: ISLLC 2008
Standard 6
An education leader promotes the success of every student by understanding, responding to, and influencing the political, social, economic, legal, and cultural environment of the school/district.

Correlated NASSP Skills: (3) sensitivity, (5) results orientation, (7) oral communication, (8) written communication

Correlated NAESP Standards: (1) balance management and leadership roles, (6) actively engage the community

Areas for ISLLC Standard 6: Political, Social, Legal, Economic, and Cultural Context

33. School Board Policy and Procedures/State and Federal Law
34. Federal Programs Administration
35. Issue and Conflict Resolution
36. Current Issues Affecting Teaching and Learning
37. Professional Affiliations and Resources
38. Professional Library

33. *School Board Policy and Procedures/State and Federal Law*

Mark an X in pencil next to the activity or activities you would like to include in your internship plan. You must choose at least ONE activity in this area, either one listed below or one your site or university supervisor approves. *You are not required to undertake every suggested activity for this area.*

A. Review the school board policy manual. Interview the superintendent or assistant superintendent, and discuss the process for creating and updating the manual. Discuss major areas that affect school principals. Include a summary of the interview in your notebook or e-portfolio.

B. Attend as many board meetings as possible. Include the agendas in your notebook or e-portfolio, as well as a list of outcomes/decisions pertaining to each agenda item and any recommendations.

C. Review board training requirements. Include a summary of board training requirements in your notebook or e-portfolio.

D. Review the board policy manual and note any policies that you are unfamiliar with or believe the school might be out of compliance with. Discuss your findings with your site supervisor. Note significant learning from the discussion and/or recommendations for additional learning on your part. Also note any recommendations regarding school compliance. Include significant learning and recommendations in your notebook or e-portfolio.

E. Perform other related activities your supervisor approves and/or service activities to the school/district your supervisor assigns and/or activities that are part of a larger project.

Context

34. *Federal Programs Administration*

Mark an X in pencil next to the activity or activities you would like to include in your internship plan. You must choose at least ONE activity in this area, either one listed below or one your site or university supervisor approves. *You are not required to undertake every suggested activity for this area.*

☐ A. Review requirements for the current Individuals with Disabilities Education Improvement Act (IDEIA), and meet with the special education director. Discuss the responsibilities of principals in meeting the guidelines. Compile a list of recommendations principals will need to meet IDEIA guidelines and better serve special-education students. Include the list in your notebook or e-portfolio.

☐ B. Attend one special-education meeting involving initial placement or an annual review. Include a critique of the meeting in your notebook or e-portfolio.

☐ C. Interview a professional responsible for career and technical education. Discuss major requirements for, concerns about, and goals of the program. Summarize these issues, and cite current and future plans to address the issues. Include the summary in your notebook or e-portfolio with recommendations for program improvement.

☐ D. Interview a professional responsible for bilingual and/or ESL programs. Discuss major requirements for, concerns about, and goals of the program. Then observe a bilingual or an ESL class; following the observation, discuss these issues with the teacher. Write a summary of the interview, observation, and discussion and include in your notebook or e-portfolio.

☐ E. Interview professionals responsible for the Gifted and At-Risk programs. Note similarities and differences in goals, processes, and issues. Solicit recommendations that principals can employ to meet the needs of both populations. Include a summary in your notebook or e-portfolio.

☐ F. Meet with a team for the Response to Intervention (RtI). Assess the current intervention procedures to support struggling learners. Who comprises the school team? How often does the team meet? Include a summary of the meeting, major issues, and concerns and recommendations in your notebook or e-portfolio.

☐ G. Perform other related activities your supervisor approves and/or service activities to the school/district your supervisor assigns and/or activities that are part of a larger project.

35. *Issue and Conflict Resolution*

Mark an X in pencil next to the activity or activities you would like to include in your internship plan. You must choose at least ONE activity in this area, either one listed below or one your site or university supervisor approves. *You are not required to undertake every suggested activity for this area.*

☐ A. Choose a current, school-related issue at your school/district. Find at least two persons on either side of the issue. Meet with the chosen persons individually or as a group to ascertain the goals for each side. Ensure that each side understands the goals of the other side. Develop a list of concerns that each side has about the opposing side. Devise a resolution that helps both sides achieve their goals and addresses all concerns. Meet with both sides to reach consensus on the new proposal or plan. Include the goals, list of concerns, and consensus on goals in your notebook or e-portfolio. Include any recommendations for the school/district concerning the issue.

☐ B. Perform other related activities your supervisor approves and/or service activities to the school/district your supervisor assigns and/or activities that are part of a larger project.

36. Current Issues Affecting Teaching and Learning

Mark an X in pencil next to the activity or activities you would like to include in your internship plan. You must choose at least ONE activity in this area, either one listed below or one your site or university supervisor approves. *You are not required to undertake every suggested activity for this area.*

☐ A. Compile a list of current issues that affect teaching and learning. Use research literature and the perspectives of administrators, teachers, students, and parents. Assess the degree of importance and urgency for each issue. Include your list and assessment with any recommendations in your notebook or e-portfolio.

☐ B. Perform other related activities your supervisor approves and/or service activities to the school/district your supervisor assigns and/or activities that are part of a larger project.

37. *Professional Affiliations and Resources*

Mark an X in pencil next to the activity or activities you would like to include in your internship plan. You must choose at least ONE activity in this area, either one listed below or one your site or university supervisor approves. *You are not required to undertake every suggested activity for this area.*

☐ A. Contact several persons experienced in the principalship, and compile a list of professional associations, service organizations, and local, state, and federal agencies that provide expertise and service to the position. Include the list of resources and their major area of service in your notebook or e-portfolio.

☐ B. Visit the NAESP or NASSP website, and compile a list of all services and information available to principals. Consider joining the relevant association (state and/or national), and begin reading periodicals and keeping up with the advances and concerns of principals across the state and/or nation. Summarize your findings and their relevance to the current needs of your school in your notebook or e-portfolio.

☐ C. Submit a brief professional development plan. It should include deficiencies cited during the internship in the various learning areas. The plan should also include ongoing development with membership in and service to pertinent organizations cited in activity B. Include the plan in your notebook or e-portfolio.

☐ D. Perform other related activities your supervisor approves and/or service activities to the school/district your supervisor assigns and/or activities that are part of a larger project.

Context

38. *Professional Library*

Mark an X in pencil next to the activity or activities you would like to include in your internship plan. You must choose at least ONE activity in this area, either one listed below or one your site or university supervisor approves. *You are not required to undertake every suggested activity for this area.*

☐ A. Compile a list of books, publications, training manuals, and district or state publications used or recommended for the principal. The list should include resources of the highest quality and relevance to the position and to education leadership. Include the list in your notebook or e-portfolio.

☐ B. Perform other related activities your supervisor approves and/or service activities to the school/district your supervisor assigns and/or activities that are part of a larger project.

2.2 Meeting with Site Supervisor

After completing Stage One and making preliminary choices of activities in the 38 skill and experience areas, meet with the site supervisor to reach consensus on a plan for the internship. The intern and site supervisor should discuss the intern's preferred activities and decide the nature of the service activities and the local project(s) described in sections 2.3 and 2.4.

2.3 Performing Service Activities

Education is a service profession. The intern should plan for appropriate modeling and accomplishments of service. The internship should balance the needs of the intern and the needs of the school/district. Both the intern and the supervisor must take care to maintain a realistic balance. The final plan should not center solely on the intern's development, and the intern's experience should not be limited by total submission to the specific needs or concerns of the school/district.

Service activities will come mainly from the site supervisor's recommendations. They can be written in the "other related activities" section listed under all the 38 leadership areas. These may be assistance with current needs and projects, assistance with day-to-day administrative duties, or other needs that the site supervisor believes will benefit the school/district and the intern.

2.4 Conducting Local Project(s)

The intern is required to conduct at least one local project. The project should be directly related to the school/district goals and related to the improvement of student performance. The project must

♦ Include other faculty or staff in a group process
♦ Be led by the intern
♦ Include a plan that describes each of the following:
   1. Need for the project
   2. Goal of the project
   3. Resources available
   4. Timeline
   5. Method of evaluation.
♦ Include other experience and skill areas, such as decision making, communication, etc.
♦ Be approved by the supervisor

The intern may choose a large project or several smaller projects. It is strongly recommended that the size and number of projects be considered with respect to time needed to fulfill other activities and current job responsibilities.

2.5 Networking

All leaders use networks to seek advice, discuss ideas, and improve their ability to fulfill the responsibilities of their positions. These networks often consist of mentors, coaches, peers, and experts in various fields. Contacts may also include community leaders, friends, and colleagues from professional and civic organizations.

After choosing skill and experience activities, service activities, and local project(s), the intern should cite key persons that he or she plans to work with, interview, and/or use for help and assistance with the internship. Resource persons should give their permission, means of communication (phone, e-mail), and times available. Some interns find it more efficient to collect and maintain a file of business cards. The documented resource network will be presented at the final internship summary report.

2.6 Organizing a Notebook or an E-Portfolio

The intern is required to obtain and use a notebook or an e-portfolio. Typically, the notebook is a large three-ring binder. Universities differ in the kinds of programs they use for e-portfolios. You will need to check with your university supervisor for that information. Interns organize their notebooks or e-portfolios with sections devoted to the 38 skill and experience areas. Some students organize with the Educational Leadership Policy Standards: ISLLC 2008. Again, consult your university supervisor to learn the requirements for organization of the notebook or e-portfolio. Keep in mind that leaders keep professional portfolios during their careers. You will choose whether to use a paper portfolio or an electronic portfolio following your internship.

2.7 Internship/Leadership Experience Overall Plan Report

In this activity, the intern will prepare and present an overall plan report. Typically, the intern will present to his or her supervisors. The report must be a professional presentation, similar to reporting to the school board. Documentation should include

- Activities planned from the 38 leadership areas
- Service activities
- Overall plan for the local project(s)
- List of resource persons to be used
- Estimated hours for the internship/leadership experience
- Estimated completion date

Implementation

3.1 Interviewing

It is highly recommended that the intern plan to schedule interviews with various school and community leaders. Interviews, however, should be only a small part of the overall experience. The intern should spend the vast majority of his or her time working rather than observing or listening. Interviewing can affect several key outcomes that the intern should consider. These include

- Meeting the right people and developing a network of experienced school leaders
- Knowing the various leadership positions and their responsibilities
- Providing the opportunity for current leaders to get to know you
- Understanding different departments and perceptions from leaders/followers within each department
- Gaining insights into better or more relevant internship activities
- Getting the "bigger picture" and having experienced mentors provide answers to questions/concerns about various areas and perspectives.

Interview Topics and Questions

- Tell me about your department/area.
- Tell me about your job duties and responsibilities.
- What are your goals?
- What are your present major concerns?
- What future concerns do you anticipate?
- What have you done to improve this school's capacity to better meet the needs of students?
- What do you need, expect, or hope for from your principal or superintendent?
- From your experience of working with your school/district, what advice would you give a new principal?

♦ What activities would you suggest I undertake during my internship to better understand and/or work with your department/area?

Add any additional questions appropriate to your knowledge/experience/project needs.

3.2 Theory into Practice: Using the 12 Major Skills

Though Kurt Lewin was right to say "there is nothing so practical as good theory," it is equally true that there is nothing so theoretical as good practice (Fullan, 2001). Hoy and Miskel (2001) conclude that theory relates to practice in three ways: theory forms a frame of reference for the practitioner, provides a general mode for analysis of practical events, and guides decision making. Wise leaders realize the need to analyze the beliefs, dispositions, traditions, and experiences that form their theories of reality and guide their practice.

This section provides a brief overview of 12 major skills for leadership development. It is intended to provide a frame of reference for the intern to reflect, practice, and assess skill development. It is assumed that the intern has previous instruction and more in-depth study in each of these areas. A list of assessment questions follows each skill overview. Use them to analyze current performance and the development of future actions (decisions) to address current problems and assist in alleviating similar problems in the future. These are the 12 skills:

1. Developing trusting relationships
2. Leading in the realization of the vision
3. Making quality decisions
4. Communicating effectively
5. Resolving conflict and issues
6. Motivating and developing others
7. Managing group processes
8. Supporting others with appropriate leadership style
9. Using power ethically
10. Creating and managing a positive culture and climate
11. Initiating change
12. Evaluating student, personnel, and program performance.

When problems occur or needs arise, people tend to focus on the immediate crisis. This focus may alleviate the current need but does little to ensure that organizational learning has occurred or similar problems will occur less often. In these situations, leaders find themselves endlessly putting out the same types of fires. Consideration of each of the 12 skills gives a leader the bigger picture and the necessary information to guide future actions for organizational improvement, heightened quality of life within the organization, increased learning, and the opportunity for developing self and others. To gather the necessary information, the leader has to ask the right questions. The analysis questions provide for a more comprehensive definition of the problem and thus allow for more appropriate actions.

Further practice on textbook cases will assist in forming the proper mental framework for viewing real-life problems or needs. With enough practice, this thinking framework becomes second nature to the leader. For optimal learning, it is advised that interns use real-life cases and cooperative learning groups. Greater learning occurs with the practice of analyzing and considering alternatives from a variety of perspectives. A sample case is provided at the end of this section to demonstrate how to analyze problems using the reflective practice of leadership skill.

1. Developing Trusting Relationships

Covey (2009) believes one thing is common to every individual and organization and that its removal will destroy the best of organizations. He adds that if it is developed, it can bring unparalleled success. That one thing is trust. Green (2011) further noted that trust affects every relationship in life and determines whether people realize their dreams. He believes that true success is impossible without trust. Trust is found in the vast majority of books on leadership to be crucial for success in leadership, if not the base of all leadership success.

Having confidence in a leader's honesty and ability has a great impact on the climate, culture, communications, and overall quality of life within an organization. Distrust breeds negativity, erases motivation, and is a major cause of turnover. Interns and new leaders must face the challenge of developing trusting relationships. Trust does not come with a title or pay scale but must be earned. An aspiring leader needs time and determined efforts to prove to others his or her reliability, honesty, and character. It can take years to earn trust, which can be erased in a moment. The wise leader understands this and begins to take actions to build and sustain trust.

These actions include being honest in every dealing with others, following through with commitments, admitting mistakes, and knowing strengths and limitations. Leaders also initiate ways to truly know others and let others truly know them. They believe in individual worth and see individuals teaching or directing the computer lab, not simply as "faculty" and "staff." They view themselves as individuals leading, not as holders of titles or roles. Being oneself does not require a role. Interns face broken relationships with other teachers as they move into administration. New administrators must form new relationships and develop new trusts. Future school leaders must research, practice, reflect, and form habits of developing and sustaining trusting relationships.

Analysis Questions for Trust

To what extent

- ♦ Has the leader relied upon or trusted others?
- ♦ Is transparent leadership modeled in the school?

♦ Has trust been established through competence, honesty, and follow-through among leadership, faculty, students, and community?

What actions are needed to address any concerns from above to solve the current problem and avoid similar problems in the future?

2. Leading in the Realization of the Vision

Of the popularly expressed requirements for leadership, one of the most common is that leaders have vision (Gardner, 1990). Research has long held that vision separates leaders from administrators or managers. An administrative manager "copes with complexity" or manages the current status quo; a leader is "coping with" and initiating change (Liphan, 1964, Kotter, 1998). Thus, managers are concerned with the efficiency of the current system; leaders look for greater effectiveness with new policies, procedures, and systems.

Leading in schools today is difficult; many teachers and parents are fearful of and resistant to change. Leading a school or district is equally difficult when only those elected have the power to change. In addition, inexperienced school administrators attempt to do things "right" and fulfill their job descriptions; they begin to behave like managers, not leaders. Realizing the vision involves risk, and few administrators are risk takers in their early years of administration.

Reducing risk and increasing the possibility of success for a vision requires all the other 11 skills. Success requires good decisions, effective communication, conflict resolution, effective motivation strategies, groups that work together, proper style and use of power, a positive culture and safe climate, an understanding of change, and effective evaluation strategies. The central ingredient for the realization of the vision is trust (Bennis and Nanus, 1985). Trust in the leader, trust in the followers, and trust in the vision can be developed only through *shared* work in all areas.

Leaders strive to move organizations and all their members to a new vision. The vision and the means to get there require understanding, effort, and support from the entire organization. Leaders do not create vision by themselves but provide the leadership for vision creation, articulation, and support. Future leaders must research, practice, reflect, and form habits of developing and working toward the realization of the vision.

Analysis Questions for Vision

To what extent

♦ Is there a clear vision of how the organization should function now and in the future? Is it shared by all?
♦ Is the mission of the organization appropriate, understood, and supported?

- ♦ Has adequate planning occurred?
- ♦ Do the vision, mission, and plans align with the key principles and beliefs of those in the organization?
- ♦ Has trust been established among leadership, faculty, students, and community?

What actions are needed to address any concerns from above to solve the current problem and avoid similar problems in the future?

3. Making Quality Decisions

Decision making is sine qua non to education administration because a school, like all formal organizations, is basically a decision-making structure (Hoy and Miskel, 2001). Decision making is a process that guides actions. Decisions are based on the beliefs, values, and previous experiences of individuals. Leaders must know themselves, know why they choose particular paths, know whom to involve, and know which particular decision-making model to use.

It is assumed that interns have deliberated on their key beliefs or principles and have some degree of understanding of the similarities and differences between themselves and others. Interns should continue to use reflection to make decisions: reflection helps people more fully understand the roots of their beliefs and the impact of those beliefs on decisions. This section will briefly review levels of involvement and the major decision-making models.

Education leadership has come a long way since the scientific management era in the early 20th century. Then, the people at the top made the decisions and believed that a rational model would shape optimal decisions. They believed they could actually know all alternatives and predict the results of each alternative. Today, researchers and theorists know better. They know that those at the top cannot accurately gather or predict all alternatives. They know that followers deserve to be involved and that input and collaboration result in better decisions. The first decision is to decide what level of involvement is most effective.

Leaders have at least four options of involvement in decisions: deciding alone, seeking participation and input, seeking collaboration, and letting others decide. These approaches are termed *autocratic, participative, collaborative,* and *laissez faire,* respectively. A wise leader uses participative and collaborative strategies for all important decisions. However, such an approach is not always possible nor it is it preferable in all situations. The leader must assess five factors to decide on the level of involvement:

1. *Time.* Urgency may require the leader make herself decision without consulting others. Participative decisions, especially collaborative decisions, require more time than a decision made alone. If important decisions are at stake, the leader must schedule more time for involvement.

2. *Staff interest in the decision.* Barnard (1938) found that individuals have a "zone of indifference" in which they simply accept the leader's decision and are apathetic toward the decision. In these cases, the leader would not benefit from trying to gain participation or collaboration. At higher levels of interest, however, more participation or collaboration is appropriate. Leaders who desire more collaboration must generate interest in the decision.

3. *Staff expertise.* Followers who have very low levels of expertise accept the decisions of leaders. Staff members who have higher levels of expertise require either participation or collaboration to arrive at successful decisions. The leader who desires collaboration must raise levels of expertise to successfully involve subordinates.

4. *Importance or need for a high-quality decision.* Some decisions are much more important and carry significant consequences. This is usually the case for instruction and learning, whether directly or indirectly. For important questions that demand high-quality decisions, collaboration is the best model. If the decision is relatively unimportant, then the leader should simply make the decision.

5. *Degree of need for buy-in or support for the decision.* Many decisions in schools need staff support for successful implementation and results. A collaborative model often increases buy-in and support.

The second decade of the 21st century is a time of empowerment and involvement in decisions. The wise leader understands that better decisions involve higher levels of involvement. This leader also understands that involvement does not simply happen or is always the best approach. Greater involvement and a collaborative (shared) decision model take time to plan, and it takes effort to educate and motivate staff to participate effectively. The resulting better decisions are worth the effort.

It should be noted that a laissez-faire model is seldom recommended. There are situations, however, in which the leader has little interest or expertise, while others on the staff do. In these rare instances, this model may be appropriate.

The effective school leader should know and be able to use a variety of decision models. The five models most often seen in research are *classical, satisficing, incremental, mixed scanning,* and *garbage can.*

1. The *classical* (also known as rational or scientific) model strives for the single best decision. It uses the traditional steps of defining the problem, gathering information, listing alternatives, predicting outcomes, and deciding on the best alternative, way to implement, and way to evaluate. As stated earlier, this sounds correct in theory, but it is difficult to implement in real life, which includes a host of unknown future events.

2. Herbert Simon (1947) examined the way administrators really made decisions. He found that leaders did not seek the best decision but a satisfactory one. If a leader can find an alternative that satisfies followers, then that is the decision to make. The use of this model, called the *satisficing* model, is situational. If the followers are highly expert and experienced, then the potential for a successful decision is high. If the others have little expertise or experience, the potential for a successful decision is limited.

3. Charles Lindblom (1959) introduced the third decision model. This model is called *incremental* (or muddling through). This option is used when a leader does not know the best solution or even any satisfactory alternative. In this circumstance, the leader takes steps similar to his or her current practice to see if improvement occurs. The main concern with this model is that the steps may or may not align with the philosophy or mission and may result in a poor decision.

4. Amitai Etzioni (1967) introduced what he believed was a union between rational and muddling through. This adaptive strategy, called *mixed scanning*, allows the leader to take steps but ensures the steps are aligned with and assist in reaching the goals of the organization. In situations with incomplete information and inadequate time, this model provides the leader with additional time and offers a possibility of finding a satisfactory decision.

5. Cohen, March, and Olsen (1972) originated the fifth model, called the *garbage can* model. Although seldom used, it is a model used before problem definition. In some situations, leaders desire to implement something that they have utilized previously. They "remove it from the garbage can" and decide to implement. Obviously, considering the model's failure to adapt to the new circumstances, new personnel, and new students, it has a high potential for failure. Although it is not recommended, the originators found that many administrators used the strategy.

Future school leaders must research, practice, reflect, and form habits of choosing the appropriate decision-making model and level of involvement.

Analysis Questions for Decision Making

To what extent:

♦ Is there a need for the decision?
♦ Were the major steps in decision making followed?
   A. Define the problem and gather information.
   B. Identify alternatives.
   C. Assess the alternatives.

    D. Select the best alternative.

    E. Accept/support the decision.

    F. Implement the decision.

    G. Evaluate the decision.

♦ Was the appropriate decision-making model used?

    A. Classical (Rational/Scientific/Optimizing)—use of major steps to find one best solution; used for narrow, simple problems with complete information and certain outcomes.

    B. Satisficing—use of major steps to find consensus (all satisfied) on solution; used with complex problems with partial information and uncertainty but with definable satisfactory outcomes and adequate time for deliberation.

    C. Incremental—choosing several alternatives and comparing results until agreement on course of action is reached; used with incomplete information, for complex problems with uncertain outcomes, without guiding policy, and during times of general organizational chaos.

    D. Mixed scanning—same as incremental, but alternatives must be aligned with mission and philosophy; used with incomplete information, for complex problems that have uncertain outcomes but with a guiding policy and mission.

    E. Garbage can—use of a previous solution to fit a current problem or no problem; used when dissatisfaction is present and solution is attractive.

♦ Was the appropriate level of involvement used?

♦ Were those affected by the decision included in the process?

What actions are needed to address any concerns from above to solve the current problem and avoid similar problems in the future?

4. Communicating Effectively

"In areas of leadership, there is no skill more essential than one's ability to communicate." (Guarino, 1974, p. 1). "Without exception, all major national school administration associations in this country stress the importance of effective communication skills." (Gorton and Snowden, 2002, p. 31). Despite these findings, schools are generally criticized for poor communication among leaders and faculty, teachers and other teachers, faculty and students, and school and community.

What is known about communication? First, it is impossible for one person to imagine a concept or an event, find the words or actions to describe (encode) it, relay these words or actions (transmit), and make another person understand (decode) the message exactly the way it was originally imagined. The difficulty of transmitting the feelings, impressions, and related experience unique to every individual only magnifies this dilemma. Leaders are responsible to continuously work toward more effective communication and better understanding among all individuals.

Second, four major communication skill areas have been identified. The first is that leaders must be proficient in giving information. This includes oral, written, and technological communication (e-mail, Web pages, Excel, PowerPoint, etc.). Leaders must develop effective two-way communication. They must also be highly proficient in the second area of communication: listening and receiving information. These two aspects of communication involve verbal and nonverbal strategies and cues. The five strongest non-verbal influences are smiles, touches, affirmative head nods, immediacy behavior (lean forward, face the individual), and eye behavior (Heintzman, et al., 1993). The successful leader develops effective verbal *and* nonverbal behaviors.

In considering both giving and receiving information, a leader should emphasize receiving information. Covey (1989) found that successful leaders seek to understand before they seek to be understood. Listening to and receiving information first allows the leader to understand the whole picture, as opposed to giving information and allowing others to know only both sides and perspectives. Carnegie (1993) teaches that no one is more persuasive than a good listener. Listening results in many other positive outcomes. These include the following:

♦ Shows interest and respect for others
♦ Allows others to vent and models appropriate social skill
♦ Increases learning and understanding of other perspectives
♦ Critical for resolution of conflict
♦ Forms the habit and appearance of wisdom
♦ Allows time for observing others' information and is sensitive to body language, inflection, emotion, etc.
♦ Allows time for listening to what the mind, heart, emotion, and body are communicating
♦ Builds rapport and meaningful relationships
♦ Develops a culture of open communication

The third aspect of effective communication is the design and management of a communication system. Ultimately, the leader is responsible for communications within and outside the organization. Without an effective system, the leader must depend on others for the accuracy and amount of information. This is often less than adequate because

♦ Others often tell a leader only what they believe the leader wants to hear.
♦ Others may tell the leader only the positive side.
♦ Others may tell the leader only the negative side.

♦ Others often omit vital information.
♦ Many do not communicate with the leader.

An effective communication system involves a variety of formats and avenues of communication. Successful leaders may regularly use meetings, surveys, interviews, group processes, suggestion boxes, needs assessments, open-door policies, the practices of walking the halls and eating in the cafeteria, and a host of others. The goal is to have several communication strategies so different people can choose the formats they like and are willing to give and receive information. The breadth of avenues and formats also allow the leader to give and receive different types of communication.

The fourth and final aspect of communication is monitoring and evaluating the first three: giving, receiving, and the system. Leaders must periodically evaluate the quantity and quality of the communication within, as well as outside, the organization. Future leaders must research, practice, reflect, and form habits of effective communication.

Analysis Questions for Communication
To what extent

♦ Did others infer my intended meaning?
♦ Have I fully understood what others are trying to say?
♦ Are people utilizing differing avenues of communication?
♦ Have I reached my entire intended audience?
♦ Is there a safe and open system for communication?

5. Resolving Conflict and Issues
Administrators face classic disagreements between individual needs and organizational expectations; consequently, they spend a substantial amount of time attempting to mediate conflict (Hoy and Miskel, 2001). In self-assessments conducted in graduate leadership classes, the authors of this text found that most students initially avoid conflict. To the novice, this makes perfect sense—who wants to be in conflict? The wise leader, however, views every conflict as an opportunity to improve organizational effectiveness, improve the quality of life for some or all of an organization's members, and better know and understand other people.

Conflict is inevitable and should warn a leader that a problem exists. Although unique situations may warrant different practices, the ideal approach is to solve problems collaboratively. Kenneth Thomas (1976) identified five styles of managing conflict: *competing, collaborating, compromising, avoiding,* and *accommodating*. Competing is similar to a directive style: a directive must be given, regardless of the competing belief. Compromising works well in the short term, but it usually does not totally resolve a conflict. Accommodating is necessary when the leader is wrong or simply willing to give in to the other side. Avoiding is seldom recommended, except for buying time for things to "cool off" or to gather additional information. Collaborating uses problem-solving strategies and is the most recommended style.

The two major areas of conflict leaders face are conflict over differing expectations of roles and differing beliefs that, if not resolved, become issues. Role conflict can take the form of the classic model developed by Gelzels (1958), in which the personal needs of individuals conflict with the needs/ expectations of the organization. These conflicts arise in numerous and varied ways. For example, the school may expect a teacher who prefers to work alone to team-teach or work with others in a group. Conflict usually occurs when individuals believe that others are acting outside of their roles or not fulfilling the expectations of their roles. One might hear, "He is not supposed to do that" or "She is not doing her job." It is imperative that leaders and followers have a mutual understanding of the expectations of the various roles within the school/district. Job descriptions and performance evaluations must align and conform to the agreed-upon expectations of particular roles.

Issue resolution is another skill essential to leadership. Issues develop when people have differing opinions or beliefs on a host of topics, such as policy, practice, goals, the means for reaching goals, values, etc. The wise leader welcomes issues and views them as an opportunity for improvement and a better understanding of all parties. As with role conflict, problem-solving approaches work best. Typically, the leader seeks consensus on the goals of either side of an issue and ensures that each side fully understands the opposing position. The leader then solicits all concerns and attempts to find a different and better solution that either side proposes. In this manner, when one side favors Plan A and the opposing side either favors Plan B or simply opposes Plan A, the leader seeks a Plan C.

Plan C is a different and better plan because it has unified goals and addresses all voiced concerns. In theory, if both sides have agreed on the goals and all concerns have been addressed, then the leader should have support from everyone. The main problems inherent in issue resolution are training staff to positively interact and "learn" from one another, being open to change (a better plan), and having a leader skilled in listening and guiding the parties to resolution.

It should be noted that this type of resolution relies on reasoning from all parties. Some positions, however, are taken without the use of reasoning. For example, some individuals are for or against sex education because of deep-seated values. Reasoning has little effect on instilled values. In other cases, positions are based on feelings, dreams, intuition, or strong "gut" feelings that override reasoning. In some instances, there is not enough information to support or predict the outcome of either side's proposed solution. In cases in which reasoning will not solve the problem, recognizing obstacles such as deep-seated values, intuitive feelings, and lack of evidence will help leaders develop more appropriate strategies for resolution. Future leaders must research, practice, reflect, and form habits of resolving conflict and issues.

Analysis Questions for Conflict and Issue Resolution
To what extent

◆ Do all persons within the organization understand the duties and responsibilities of his or her position and the positions of others?
◆ Are expectations for others realistic and aligned with job descriptions?
◆ Is conflict seen as an opportunity?
◆ Have steps been taken to resolve personal conflict and/or issue conflict? Have steps moved both sides toward a different and better solution (versus defensive argument of current positions)?

What actions are needed to address any concerns from above to solve the current problem and avoid similar problems in the future?

6. Motivating and Developing Others

No human venture succeeds without strongly motivated men and women (Gardner, 1990). The wise leader understands that there is no universal motivation for every individual but seeks to discover what motivates the people that he or she leads. There are many theories on motivation, and each theory may partly apply to some people. The following brief overview of some major theories is presented for the intern to consider for better understanding and use.

Before presenting theories for consideration and use, one should note what not to consider or use. There is a deep tradition of behavioral thinking in public schools. For all practical purposes, most psychologists do not accept or use behavioral theories in their practices. The field has moved past Pavlov and Skinner, who believed that the key to increasing motivation is providing consistent and appropriate consequences to reinforce desired behaviors. Kohn challenged the reliance on rewards to motivate individuals in his provocative book *Punished by Rewards* (1993). He contends that hundreds of studies have shown that rewards produce only temporary compliance and that no lasting change in attitudes or behaviors can be attributed to the use of rewards. Cameron and Pierce used meta-analysis to assess the impact of reward as studied by all research performed since the 1970s and concluded that rewards are not inherently bad or good for people. Control over others and the manipulation of reality is inappropriate and unethical. Unfortunately, many school leaders wonder, "What rewards and punishments can we use to induce others to act appropriately?" Leaders need to move from behavioral perspectives to cognitive ones.

One cognitive theory is Attribution Theory, developed by Weiner (1986). Attribution Theory is simply based on exactly what an individual attributes to his or her success or failure. When something happens, an individual can make two explanations for it: an external attribution or an internal attribution. An external attribution assigns causality to an outside agent or force, and an internal attribution assigns causality to factors within the person. Attribution Theory contends that high achievers attribute their successes and failures to factors within themselves and their control. The key to improving motivation, according to Attribution Theory is to help people develop self-attribution explanations of effort for their success or failure.

Cognitive Dissonance Theory, proposed by Festinger (1957) details ideas similar to the disequilibrium described by Piaget's theory of cognitive development. Festinger's theory states that when there is a discrepancy between two beliefs, two actions, or a belief and an action, people will act to resolve the conflict and discrepancies. To motivate people to act, one must create the appropriate amount of disequilibrium.

Expectancy Theory, attributed to Vroom, proposes the following equation to determine motivation: motivation = perceived probability (expectancy) × connection of success and reward (instrumentality) × value of obtaining the goal (valance/value). The equation details the idea that motivation is the product of a person's belief that he or she can succeed at a task, the degree of connection that he or she sees between the activity and success, and how much he or she values the results of success. All three variables must be high for an individual to be motivated.

Maslow (1954) developed the Hierarchy of Human Needs to detail his theory of human motivation. Maslow contends that individuals have hierarchies of needs that motivate their behavior. People are motivated to attend to and satisfy their needs for physiological satisfaction, safety, belonging and love, self-esteem, and self-actualization. Individuals are motivated to satisfy these needs in this order. The leader's responsibility is to provide for lower level needs and assist members of the organization to reach higher levels.

Alderfer (1972) developed a hierarchy of three human needs. These needs included the basic need for existence, the need for relatedness, and the need for growth. Alderfer, like Maslow, contended that individuals are inherently motivated to satisfy these needs and that organizations and schools should work to ensure that many of their employees' and students' needs are met to ensure proper motivation.

William Glasser (1985) identified five basic needs: the need for belonging, power, fun, freedom, and survival. The need for belonging is described as the need for involvement with people, the need to love and be loved, and to affiliate and bond with other people. The need for power is described as the need for achievement and accomplishment—a sense of being in control of one's own life. The need for fun is the need to enjoy life, laugh, and see humor. The need for freedom is the need to make choices and live without undue restraint. The need for survival is the need to maintain life and good health, including the basic needs of comfort, food, shelter, water, etc.

Fredrick Herzberg (1959) proposed the Motivation and Hygiene Theory, which organizes elements that determine an organization's ability to motivate its employees into two sections: hygiene and motivational issues. Herzberg contends that hygiene issues can't motivate employees but can minimize dissatisfaction. Hygiene issues include policies, supervision, salary, interpersonal relations, and working conditions. Motivators create satisfaction by fulfilling individuals' needs for meaning and personal growth. Herzberg identified achievement, recognition, the work itself, responsibility, and advancement as individual motivators. The best way to help motivate people is to ensure that both hygiene and motivational issues and needs are met.

Bandura (1986) proposed reciprocal determination as a primary factor in both learning and motivation. He believed that the environment (an individual's behavior) and the individual's characteristics (an individual's knowledge, emotions, and cognitive development) both influence and are influenced by each other. Two components of Bandura's Social Cognition Theory affect an individual's learning and motivation. The components are self-efficacy and self-regulation. Self-efficacy involves a person's belief that a particular action is possible and that he or she can successfully accomplish the action. Self-regulation involves the person's ability to establish goals, to develop a plan to attain the goals, to display the commitment needed to implement the plan, and to reflect on and modify the plan if needed. To increase motivation, one must provide for and support another's self-efficacy and self-regulatory needs. The more individuals believe they will be successful, and the better able they are to regulate their goals and plans, the more motivated they will be.

McClelland (1961), in his Achievement Motivation Theory, asserted three basic motivational human needs: achievement, power, and affiliation. McClelland's need for achievement includes an individual's need for feedback, the need to take moderate risks, the need for personal responsibility, and the need for success. The need for power is rooted in an individual's need for influence over his own life and others. An individual's need for affiliation is based on the human needs for acceptance, friendship, and love and his or her desire to cooperate with others. The leader's responsibility is to provide for all three but to focus on achievement.

Ames (1992) and Maehr and Midgley (1991) also focused on achievement motivation with their Goal Theory. The Goal Theory of Motivation states that the reasons or purposes an individual perceives for achievement determine success. The theory identifies two types of goals: task goals and ability goals. When pursuing task goals, an individual focuses on mastering skills and knowledge, and the motivation is personal improvement or understanding. When pursuing ability goals, a person focuses on appearing competent, and the motivation is to demonstrate one's ability. Goal theorists have recommended that schools work toward task goals and away from ability goals in classrooms. They propose that schools move away from recognition for relative performance, honor rolls for high grades, and the overuse of praise. To motivate students, schools should move toward the recognition of progress improvement and emphasize learning for its own sake.

The intern must be knowledgeable about motivation theory and attempt to increase motivation. Rewards and coercive behavior modification may show temporary results but may cause harm. The key is to understand what motivates each member of the organization. Future leaders must research, practice, reflect, and form habits of providing for motivation for everyone they lead.

Analysis Questions for Motivation
To what extent

- Are people's needs being met?
- Are people's needs in line with the needs of the organization?
- Are differing processes used to motivate? Are they effective?
- Are varying methods used to develop others?

What actions are needed to address any concerns from above to solve the current problem and avoid similar problems in the future?

7. Managing Group Processes

Warren Bennis (2000) believes that contemporary American society is the product of "Great Groups," teams of creative persons who banded together to achieve remarkable successes that would not have been possible through a traditional hierarchical approach. Research on group processes in schools has shown that leaders who trust and believe in others and model these traits accomplish far more and develop devoted followers (Hoyle, English, & Steffy, 1990). But if success in leadership is defined as "the ability to get groups of people to work toward the accomplishment of the vision, mission, and goals for the district/school," most education leaders would not meet the definition. Traditionally, schools are organizations in which work is done individually.

Breaking with this tradition and reforming the culture in which faculty and administrators collaboratively work toward school improvement requires commitment to empowerment, the development of new leaders, cooperation, and shared responsibility. Leaders must invest time, effort, and expertise to overcome traditions, past failures, and lack of interest and/or expertise on the part of faculty (and administrators) to work together.

Teachers in graduate education leadership programs often admit to very negative perspectives and past experiences with teams, committees, and groups. "All they wanted us to do was to come up with what they wanted in the first place." "We worked very hard, and then they did not accept our recommendation." "They refuse to listen to any problem or complaint." "Why should we do their job?" "We have enough to do without doing extra work." Overcoming these negative attitudes is a difficult, but not impossible, task.

The intern should remember that to change an attitude, one must change a belief. To change a belief, one must experience something new. Thus, it is the responsibility of the leader to provide new, positive experiences in working in groups and sharing goals, responsibility, authority, and decision making. Many studies on group work describe how leaders should conduct meetings and train staff to work in groups.

Meetings should be called only when there is a need to meet. Calling in the entire faculty to announce something that could be communicated in writing is insulting and a waste of time. In such an instance, there is no need to meet. Calling a meeting to discuss the failures of a few faculty members wastes the time of all the others. Deciding whether to schedule a meeting should be based on common sense. Meetings involve discussion, group learning, group thinking, and group work. Obviously, a leader should develop a set of principles or rules for meetings and use effective skills to conduct meetings.

The following is an example of rules for meetings:

♦ Schedule meetings only when necessary and people need to meet. It is advised, however, that the leader not go for long periods without meeting with staff. Information that can be put in writing should be communicated through e-mail, memos, or other means of two-way communication between meetings.

♦ Prior to a meeting, distribute an agenda with the purpose, time, and location listed. Participants in meetings should come prepared and have read or considered items to be discussed in the meeting. The leader should give staff the opportunity to request items for the agenda. The leader should allow time to decide or discuss additions to the agenda. It is important that all faculty members know that they have a say in their meetings and that their input is valued.

♦ Meetings should be arranged and organized for participation. The leader may use a circle or semicircle or at least stand or sit on the same level.

♦ The leader should solicit participation from and show interest in individual members. He or she should model listening skills and value comments from and conflicting perspectives of the members.

♦ The leader should stay on time and on task. Often, a leader plans for more than can be accomplished at one meeting. Thus, time management is vital, and the leader is responsible for keeping to the item or task at hand. It is also the responsibility of the leader to begin and end on time. Most staff developers recommend ending meetings a few minutes early. People tend to quit listening if meetings go beyond the scheduled ending time. It is also poor modeling for the leader to keep meetings past the announced time.

♦ The leader summarizes accomplishments of the meeting and follows up on decisions. Followers quickly lose respect and trust in leaders who speak well but do not follow up. Followers expect meetings to produce results. Follow-up is crucial in establishing a culture in which meetings are viewed as important and productive.

In addition to attending leader-called meetings, faculty members meet at other times. They may go to grade-level or subject-area department meetings, committee meetings, task force meeting, or a host of other types of meetings. If the leader expects these meetings to be productive, participants must receive training. Members need guidelines, adequate information, a clear understanding of purposes and goals, and the ability to work in a group. A group may have an assigned leader, such as a department chair, or a task may be assigned, and a leader may emerge. Often, different faculty members have different expertise and skills, and different leaders may emerge for different topics or tasks.

Regardless of the type of meeting or whether a leader is assigned, members of the group need to formalize their own set of rules. How much time will participants spend? Do participants need goal consensus and/or consensus on the final recommendation? Are participants meeting to learn more about the topic and one another, or are they present to argue and defend their opinions? Is interrupting and judging others' comments allowed? Do participants agree to share responsibility equally? Productive groups do not just happen; they must be developed.

As previously written, great things can be accomplished by getting groups of people to work together. The time and effort the leader spends to develop this type of culture pays great dividends in the long term. To overcome many negative attitudes about meetings, committees, and working groups, the leader must truly believe in others and their abilities to accomplish tasks and make effective decisions. Leaders should never pretend to give groups responsibility or authority, and leaders should always be completely honest. It is imperative that future school leaders research, practice, reflect, and form habits of effective group processes to solicit support, develop new leaders, and reach organizational goals.

Analysis Questions for Group Processes
To what extent

+ Have the formal and informal groups been identified?
+ Do all groups work productively and collaboratively?
+ Are goals for the groups realistic, understood, and acceptable?
+ Is trust and freedom of expression the norm of all groups?
+ Are meetings used effectively and efficiently?

What actions are needed to address any concerns from above to solve the current problem and avoid similar problems in the future?

8. Supporting Others with Appropriate Leadership Style
For decades, researchers have studied leadership style. They have coined many terms to describe leadership style. Dunn and Dunn (1977) listed seven

styles: collaborative, cooperative, participative, bureaucratic, laissez-faire, benevolent despot, and autocratic. More recently, Goleman (2000) devised six terms that described various styles business leaders use : coercive, commanding, affiliative, democratic, pacesetting, and coaching. He found coercive and pacesetting negative and the other four positive.

In combination of these and others, this text offers six styles to consider for appropriate use:

1. *Directive*. Similar to authoritative, autocratic, or commanding, this style is used when strict compliance is needed or the situation is urgent or an emergency. The directive style is appropriate for quick changes or guidance. It is also appropriate when only the leader has the necessary knowledge or expertise to make the decision.

2. *Participative*. Often labeled democratic, this style is used when limited time is available and/or the leader holds most of the accountability for the results. With this style, the leader makes the final decision or approves policy or practice but gathers input from others. Ideally, this involves all those affected by the decision or action.

3. *Collaborative*. Also labeled democratic, this is the ideal style and is a means of working in true collaboration with others. This style values others' expertise and helps develop future leaders. Using this style requires adequate time, training, and shared responsibility. In most cases, collaboration results in better decisions.

4. *Coaching*. The leader remains in a leader/teacher/mentor role with subordinates This is an ideal style when followers are not prepared for true collaboration. Coaching frees subordinates to practice as leaders, under the guidance and observation of the leader.

5. *Affiliative*. This style is appropriate when the leader has more concern for the person or persons than the task. The leader could be trying to build positive relationships, or personnel could be dealing with personal issues. When the personal problem passes or the relationship has been formed, the leader can focus on the task and use a coaching or collaborative style. It should be noted that this is the opposite of Goleman's pacesetting style, in which the task takes precedence over people.

6. *Laissez-faire*. This style is seldom recommended but may be appropriate for minor tasks when followers have more expertise and interest than the leader.

The key to using the most effective style is to know the situation and people and strive to meet the needs of both. In some cases, the entire staff must be dealt with using a very directive style; at other times, only some staff members will need a directive style. In some cases, some staff may need coaching, while others are prepared to collaborate. The main lesson is that people and situations, not the leader's preferences, dictate what style the leader should use.

Analysis Questions for Leadership Style

To what extent has the appropriate style been used with differing people?

1. Directive (authoritarian, commanding)—legal mandate; very little time, interest and/or expertise among followers; low need for quality and/or support for decision; greater need for task than for people
2. Participative (democratic)—limited time, limited expertise of leader, limited interest and/or expertise of followers, some degree of quality and support needed
3. Collaborative (democratic, shared decision making)—adequate time; high degree of interest and expertise among followers; high need for quality and support; desire for developing followers
4. Coaching—adequate time; need to increase interest and expertise among followers; desire to develop followers and future leaders; need for support and assistance to individuals; higher need for people than for task
5. Affiliative—total concern for needs of people rather than task
6. Laissez-faire (complete delegation)—adequate time; high degree of interest and expertise among followers; low level of interest and/or expertise of leader; low need for quality of decision; desire to let others lead.

What actions are needed to address any concerns from above to solve the current problem and avoid similar problems in the future?

9. Using Power Ethically

A leader must wield power to accomplish great things. Although many believe power corrupts or that no person should have power over another, power can be both positive and negative. The wise leader understands the negative potential of power but strives to use power for good. In the classic model of power, French and Raven (1959) believe there are five basic types of power: reward, coercive, legitimate, referent, and expert.

The use of *reward power* is tempting. Many believe it is right to reward others for their effort and feel a sense of joy in giving to those who deserve it. However, the use of reward power can do more harm than good. If some receive rewards, others are overlooked. Some who receive rewards begin to expect them and may work only for rewards or limit their efforts to the criteria set for rewards. In addition, finding a reward that everyone is willing to work for is impossible. The reward system becomes a "game," and many tire of playing. The result is that the leader's power is diminished. Use of reward power is not recommended.

Coercive power is an obvious misuse of power. Yet coercive power is often used with students. Threatening children for misbehavior or poor academic performance carries over to administration, and threats are then made to faculty and staff. The use of coercive power is unethical. Coercion and punishment do not solve problems in schools. The wise leader refrains from using either reward or coercive power.

Legitimate power derives from the authority of the position. Superintendents have authority over principals; principals have authority over teachers; and teachers have authority over students. Depending on the history and culture of the school/district, however, the power given to a position may vary. Some teachers have very little power over students, and some principals exert minimal power over the faculty. Others give power to the leader, so he or she cannot depend solely on the power of the position.

The wise leader understands both the powers inherent to the position and the powers *not* given to the position. As previously mentioned in role conflict, it is vital for the leader to act within the laws, policies, and traditions of his or her position. Abuse of power causes conflict, and refusal to use power is a failure to fulfill the responsibilities of the position. The leader is responsible for knowing and acting within the appropriate range of legitimate power or authority.

So far, this text has recommended not using two types of power and recommended the limited use of another. Leaders who desire additional power to accomplish great things must seek to expand their referent and/or expert power.

Referent power is the ideal. Followers give power to leaders whom they identify with, believe in, and trust. To increase referent power, the leader must know others and allow them to know him or her. The leader must work with others, find consensus in the vision, and determine the means of achieving the vision. Gaining referent power requires effective communication and a strong belief in the value of others and working together.

Possessing special knowledge or skill creates expert power. Followers freely give power to experts for help and guidance. To increase expert power, the leader must commit time and effort to become more expert in essential areas of leadership and education. These may include expertise in curriculum, technology, instruction, school operations, communication, and a host of other possibilities. The wise leader seeks additional expertise in all areas but focuses on the greatest strengths and needs of others.

It should be noted that the omission of political power is purposeful. Political power is power derived from the exchange of favors for personal gain. Although every organization has some degree of political activity, the wise leader does not seek personal gain but rather gain for others and the organization. The term *political leadership* is an oxymoron. The intern must be aware of politics, so as not to be abused by it, but avoid seeking political power or taking any leadership position solely for personal gain.

The final aspect of power is empowerment. Most of the research today recommends teacher empowerment (Rice and Schneider, 1994; Marks and Louis, 1997; Rinehart, Short, and Johnson, 1997; Rinehart, Short, Short, and Eckley, 1998). The wise leader understands that empowering others in the quest for school improvement builds a broad power base. One who gives power gains power. Only in politics would one view this as giving up power. Empowering others builds support, buy-in, and consensus and the development of current and future leaders. It is imperative that future school leaders research, practice, reflect, and form habits of using appropriate style and power to reach organizational goals and positively and ethically meet the needs of everyone they lead.

Analysis Questions for Power

To what extent

- Has the leader exerted the good use of referent or expert power?
- Has the leader exerted the misuse of coercive or reward power?
- Are duties and power delegated in the organization?
- Do faculty, students, and parents feel empowered?

What actions are needed to address any concerns from above to solve the current problem and avoid similar problems in the future?

10. Creating and Managing a Positive Culture and Climate

The only things of real importance that leaders do is create and manage culture (Schein, 1992). This is best understood when one considers that a school's vision, ways of making decisions and communicating, amount and type of conflict, degree of motivation, use of power, and ability to change are all ingredients of its culture. People form attitudes toward (Greenberg and Baron, 1997) or ideologies (Mintzberg, 1989) of the values, norms, expectations, and practices that set their school apart from others. The culture also includes the history, traditions, and beliefs of the organization and the relative importance of each.

The leader is responsible for understanding the culture. He or she realizes that culture changes over time and that subcultures exist. The wise leader assesses the past and current culture and seeks consensus for improvement. Cultural changes take time, need a shared commitment, and require extensive follow-up to become an accepted aspect of the new culture.

Leaders can use formal assessments from business or principal organizations, for example, the National Association for Secondary School Principals and/or National Association of Elementary School Principals. Or they can assess current needs or issues. How does the organization promote diversity, support staff development, recognize progress, and invite parent involvement? What beliefs underlie these issues? Do the policies and practices align with the mission? What can be learned from other schools in the United States and abroad? Once the culture is understood, steps can be taken to improve it.

Studies indicate that the most effective schools are distinguished by outstanding social climates—not by elaborate facilities, extensively trained teachers, small classes, or high levels of financial support (Erickson, 1981). School climate is simply defined as the feelings or atmosphere of the school. Climate can change quickly and often. The leader must always be aware of the climate and take action if the current climate is negative.

The leader should be proactive in dealing with climate. The leader can use formal assessments, develop trusting relationships, have effective means for communicating, and be aware of the feelings and atmosphere on a daily basis. The leader should be very sensitive to and take responsibility for staff and student morale. He or she should investigate the causes for low morale and the steps that can be taken to raise morale.

Climate and culture are extremely important aspects for measuring the "quality of life" in the school. Quality of life affects academic performance, behavior, staff turnover, motivation, physical health, and the mental health of all members of the school. Future leaders must research, practice, reflect, and form habits of assessing, improving, and creating a positive school culture and climate.

Analysis Questions for Culture and Climate
To what extent

- ♦ Are there conflicts/concerns with the current organizational culture?
- ♦ If conflicts exist, have adequate time and resources been allocated to developing a new culture?
- ♦ Are there concerns with the current climate?
- ♦ Have adequate assessments been conducted to accurately assess the climate?

What actions are needed to address any concerns from the previous page to solve the current problem and avoid similar problems in the future?

11. Initiating Change
Successful leaders initiate and manage change. Of all of the skills presented in this text, leading change is the most difficult. Fullan (2001) asserts that there are two main aspects of education change: what changes to implement (theories of education) and how to implement change (theories of change). They interact and shape each other, but the critical factor is the distinctiveness of the individual setting. What works in one setting may not work in another.

What is known about change?

- It is a process that takes place over time (two to three years).
- The process has steps or stages and requires a change in belief.
- Change must begin with individuals, then spread out to the organization.
- Change is difficult and seldom worth the effort; most changes fail.
- A real need or pressure is required and not everyone will change.
- No amount of information will make the change totally clear.
- Change will always involve disagreement and conflict.
- The leader plays a key role in facilitating change.
- Those affected by change must be involved in the process.
- It must be evaluated and monitored from beginning to end.
- Improvement cannot occur without change.

The most startling aspect of the list above is that most change efforts fail. Most experts recommend attempting only one or two changes at a time. The wise leader must fully understand the change process and choose his or her change efforts carefully. Most people fear and/or resist change. Change causes disequilibrium in individuals, and they seek the balance of the past.

What are the factors in resistance to change?

- Some people agree with new programs but never do anything.
- Some need more time—they rationalize resistance.
- Some are against any change made at a state or national level.
- Some consider only costs—is the change worth the time and effort?
- Some only want incremental change and fear large change efforts.
- Some people are successful in terms of maintaining the status quo and are very conservative toward change.
- Some lack the skill to make the change or have an honest difference of opinion.

Leaders can take appropriate actions to reduce resistance in spite of these factors. These include the following:

- Help teachers feel the change is their own.
- Show that the change reduces rather than increases their burdens.
- Involve others and reach consensus on the value of the change.
- Validate and recognize objections, and give feedback and clarification.
- Develop support, trust, and confidence of those involved.
- Set attainable and realistic goals, and be open to revision and improvement.
- Change and resistance to change are inevitable; the leader must guide and direct change.

Factors that determine successful change efforts:

♦ Ownership is broad-based and includes informal and formal power.
♦ Positive relationships are built.
♦ The administration supports change, and the community is aware of the change.
♦ The change fits the philosophy, mission, and culture of the school.
♦ The moral purpose is relevant to those affected.
♦ Plans, evaluations, and adequate resources are available.
♦ Monitoring and adjustment occur in the process.
♦ Substantial training occurs during the implementation phase.
♦ Few, if any, other big changes occur at the same time.

These lists were compiled from the works of Evans (1996); Hendricks and Ludeman (1996), Senge et al. (1996), Wagner (1994), Hall and Hord (2001), and Fullan (2002). It should be noted that the lack of any one variable might cause the change to fail.

It has been said that change is the only constant in life. It has also been said that everyone wants improvement, but no one wants change. The skill of effecting change requires much thought, analysis, and effort. Despite the hurdles, if one is to lead, one must lead change. Future leaders must research, practice, reflect, and form habits of leading education change.

Analysis Questions for Change

To what extent

♦ Is the proposed change only one of a few?
♦ Does the change have a moral purpose?
♦ Do all involved understand the change process?
♦ Have positive relationships been built?
♦ Is creating and sharing information a priority?
♦ Has a productive disturbance and a subsequent coherence been accomplished?
♦ Have steps been taken to reduce resistance?
♦ Have the factors that produce success been implemented?

What actions are needed to address any concerns from above to solve the current problem and avoid similar problems in the future?

12. Evaluating Student, Personnel, and Program Performance

The topic of evaluation is complex, controversial, and involves many entities, subjects, criteria, and beliefs. The federal government, unions, accrediting agencies, boards of education, universities, real estate agencies, the media, and a host of professional organizations all rate and evaluate public schools. One might conclude that so many others get involved because educators do a poor job of it.

Anything worth doing is worth evaluating and finding improvements for. Only through meaningful, valid, and reliable evaluation can strengths, weaknesses, conflicting efforts, and wasteful efforts emerge and allow leaders to analyze and take appropriate actions. Ratings and labeling do little to find answers. Evaluation must be thorough and have adequate breadth and depth.

Evaluations should be administered for the following:

♦ Faculty, staff, and students
♦ Recruiting, hiring, and developing and retaining staff
♦ Programs and co-curricular activities
♦ Curriculum, instruction, and testing
♦ Technology
♦ Community and parent relations
♦ Food service, transportation, facilities, and safety
♦ Fiscal accountability and legal compliance
♦ All 12 leadership skills.

This list is not exhaustive, but it does show the scope of what needs evaluation. Only through evaluative information can leaders plan appropriate action for improvement. An evaluation must begin with the existing practice and measure the extent of progress toward the vision or final goal. Beginning, formative, and summative measures should be taken at appropriate intervals. Care must be taken to choose evaluative instruments that reliably measure what the leader intends to measure.

The new bandwagon in education leadership is making data-driven decisions. Many new books are available to help leaders improve skills in collecting, analyzing, and using data to make plans and decisions. It is highly recommended that future leaders study and develop new skills in the use of evaluative data to increase learning and the overall performance of schools.

Analysis Questions for Evaluation
To what extent

♦ Are effective personnel and program evaluations established?
♦ Are both formative and summative evaluations utilized?
♦ Is data from evaluations used for decisions and planning?

What actions are needed to address any concerns from above to solve the current problem and avoid similar problems in the future?

Sample Case

The following, relatively minor, case is presented to show how the previous analysis questions can be used to find weaknesses in leadership skill and make recommendations for professional development and school improvement.

What Not to Wear

Ted Smith was in his first year teaching eighth grade at Southwest Middle School. He had six years of previous teaching experience at another school with very good evaluations. He was popular with the students but had little interaction with other teachers. He set high expectations, and his students scored higher than the district average on various normed and criteria-referenced tests. He appeared to enjoy teaching at Southwest and never voiced complaints.

In January, four other eighth-grade teachers went to the principal's office with concerns about Mr. Smith's clothing. The principal, Mrs. White, was surprised to see the teachers so upset and frustrated with the situation. They reported that they had observed Mr. Smith coming to school most days wearing jeans, T-shirts, and sneakers. They felt he failed to meet the policy that required "appropriate and professional dress." They wanted to know why the principal had allowed this to continue.

Mrs. White said that she knew Mr. Smith did not dress as nicely as most others but that he appeared to dress neatly, and she had never received any complaints before. The teachers remarked that they had heard complaints from many others and that his dress was unprofessional and embarrassing. They

felt he was a poor model for the students and should not be given a new contract unless his dress met the policy. One teacher reminded the principal that she had made many comments about following policy during the year. The teacher did not understand why Mr. Smith was allowed to ignore policy. Mrs. White said she would meet with Mr. Smith at the end of the day to discuss the matter.

Before reviewing the analysis on the following pages, consider what you would do.

It should be noted that when experienced administrators reviewed this case, many simply said to call in Mr. Smith and inform him that his dress style must change and meet written policy—case closed, on to the next one. Keep in mind that although this case appears to be more of a management issue than a leadership or instructional issue, if problems are found in decisions, communication, groups working together, culture, etc., these are all necessary skills for increasing learning and therefore, must be addressed.

Consider whether the following analysis provides better information and leads to more appropriate actions than your initial reaction. The following analysis incorporated the questions from each skill area. Many of the areas of analysis overlap with others. For example, improper style, decision making, or communication can cause conflict and/or decrease motivation—each area affects other areas. Thus, there is overlap in defining the problem and considering actions to take. The leader must summarize and prioritize data collected from the analysis and then plan appropriate action.

Trust

Aspects of the problem found:

- ♦ Little trust by the other teachers that the principal would take action
- ♦ No evidence of trusting relationships among eighth-grade teachers

Actions to take:

- ♦ Follow through on the promise to meet with Mr. Smith and correct the problem.
- ♦ Ensure that all faculty members understand the definition of professional dress and the actions the principal will take if policy is not met.
- ♦ Set up meetings with the eighth-grade teachers for sharing ideas, concerns, and goals. Create opportunities for the teachers to get know one another better.

Vision

Aspects of the problem found:

- ♦ No clear, shared vision about how the staff should dress
- ♦ No shared understanding of the definition of "appropriate and professional"
- ♦ Currently no plans to address professional dress
- ♦ A sense of distrust among some teachers about whether the principal enforces policy uniformly

Actions to take:

- ♦ Choose a participatory or collaborative strategy to gather information for consensus on appropriate and professional dress.
- ♦ Include an interpretation of the definition of appropriate dress in the Teacher Handbook.

- ♦ Meet with or survey staff about other concerns in policy that the principal should address.
- ♦ Follow up with the teachers to develop a higher degree of trust.

Decision making

Aspects of the problem found:

- ♦ There is no clear knowledge about the extent of the problem. Are other teachers concerned? Besides Mr. Smith, are there others who do not meet policy?
- ♦ There is no information about whether failure to adhere to policy affects learning.
- ♦ No alternatives for dealing with Mr. Smith are generated.
- ♦ What decision–making model should be used?
- ♦ How many people should be involved?

Actions to take:

- ♦ Meet with members of diverse formal and informal groups to ascertain the extent and magnitude of the problem.
- ♦ Because staff has a high level of interest in and expertise about dress and buy-in is needed, use the satisficing model and seek consensus through collaboration.
- ♦ Because this affects all staff, include all staff in the collaboration.
- ♦ Provide adequate time for staff to reach consensus.

Communication

Aspects of the problem found:

- ♦ The policy lacks needed detail and/or the leader has not clarified the policy.

- The concern has bothered staff for many months but was not voiced before—why?
- What other concerns are present and not reported to the principal?
- The principal and staff do not agree with/understand the policy in the same way.

Actions to take:

- Ensure that the policy includes adequate detail.
- Communicate both orally and in writing the expectations for staff attire.
- Take steps to inform staff of your desire and expectation to hear concerns.
- Provide various avenues for soliciting concerns; for example, meet with departments on a regular basis, take time to visit with staff and students before and after school, and promote an open-door policy.
- Assess the level of communication between yourself and staff, and work to create a more effective network.

Conflict

Aspects of the problem found:

- The roles of the principal and teachers in addressing policy issues are misunderstood.
- There is no clear expectation about how teachers should voice concerns.
- The teachers view the issue as embarrassing, not an opportunity for improvement.
- No steps are taken to resolve conflict between teachers.

Actions to take:

- Clarify and communicate the roles the principal and teachers play in resolving policy issues.

- Elaborate to staff your desire to hear and address concerns about improvements to the school and each of its members.
- Provide staff development for conflict resolution at the personal and departmental levels.
- Gather as many alternatives as possible before making a decision.
- Model conflict resolution for staff.

Motivation

Aspects of the problem found:

- The needs of the eighth-grade teachers are not being met.
- Mr. Smith's needs are not in line with organizational needs.
- Mr. Smith does not appear to belong to any faculty groups.
- A mentor or buddy system for new teachers is not in place.

Actions to take:

- Use the satisficing model, and seek consensus to ensure that needs are met and aligned with the organization's needs and expectations.
- Plan for all staff to be part of formal or informal groups.

Group Processes

Aspects of the problem found:

- Is Mr. Smith in an informal group? If not, why?
- Does Mr. Smith participate in the formal eighth-grade group? If not, why?
- Is professionalism one of its goals of the eighth-grade faculty?
- The eighth-grade teachers have not developed trust and openness to discuss concerns.
- How often does the eighth-grade faculty meet? Are the meetings run effectively?

♦ Have the eighth-grade teachers been trained in leading and being members of a group?

Actions to take:
♦ Meet with Mr. Smith, and discuss communication and collaboration with other eighth-grade teachers and staff.
♦ Provide training for the grade-level or department chair in leading meetings.
♦ Provide training for others in being effective group members and developing mutual trust.

Leadership Style
Aspects of the problem found:
♦ Teachers want the principal to use a directive style with an experienced teacher.

Actions to take:
♦ Begin by using the coaching or democratic leadership style with Mr. Smith, and ascertain whether this is successful. If not, you may need to use the directive style until a more positive relationship is built.
♦ Strive for additional referent (shared beliefs, values) power and/or expert power in communications, decisions, and group processes.

Power
Aspects of the problem found:
♦ Teachers display very little degree of power in resolving the issue with Mr. Smith.

Actions to take:
♦ Meet with the eighth-grade teachers, and reach consensus about expectations and the power to

confront one another is grade-level meetings.

Culture/Climate
Aspects of the problem found:
♦ Lack of a culture of open communications
♦ Lack of a culture of professionalism in dress
♦ At present, no time or resources devoted to issue
♦ Climate of frustration and ill feeling among some eighth-grade teachers
♦ No assessments on climate available or scheduled

Actions to take:
♦ Meet with faculty, and discuss the desire and necessity for open communication.
♦ Meet to develop consensus about professional dress.
♦ Take extra time and make extra efforts to meet the needs of the concerned eighth-grade teachers.
♦ Plan periodic assessments of the school climate, and take measures to address any concerns.

Change
Aspects of the problem found:
♦ None

Actions to take:
♦ No major change efforts planned

Evaluation
Aspects of the problem found:
♦ Adequate information about clothing policy is not part of hiring or induction practices.
♦ Periodic assessments of climate, concerns, and needs are not conducted.

Actions to take:

♦ Review hiring information, and ensure that policy concerning professional dress and adequate details about the policy are included.

♦ Develop and use assessments at the beginning, middle, and end of the year to include measurements on climate, communication, and any other issues deemed important to staff and students.

A manager might simply decide to tell Mr. Smith to dress according to policy. An education leader, however, would be very concerned with developing Mr. Smith because he appears to be an effective teacher. The leader would also want the eighth-grade teachers to work more effectively together—a skill needed to improve instruction and increase learning. The leader would also focus on increasing his or her skill in any other areas that surface as needing improvement. Keeping the focus on changes to increase learning, improve the overall school, and develop self and others is one difference between managers and leaders. The intern should focus on leading, not managing. Develop your skills and keep the proper focus.

Interns are expected to assess, monitor, and utilize ongoing reflection on and evaluation of their skill development. Although skill development is essential for success in school leadership, reflection is imperative for knowledge, disposition, and the ethical beliefs that guide actions. Skill without knowledge, appropriate disposition, or ethical belief will do little to develop others and meet the learning and developmental needs of students. The next sections will assist the intern with ongoing reflection and evaluation.

3.3 Reflection in Action

In writing this section, the authors assume that reflection is built into all of the assignments in the book and also into the coursework that students will complete throughout their graduate programs. We believe it will be helpful to define reflection and reflective practices in order to understand how reflection is part of administrative learning.

Defining Reflection and Reflective Practice

Reflection means looking at practice systematically. Interns who aspire to be principals and administrators need to understand how reflection is different from other types of thought. When people look at evidence of reflection and reflective skills, what do they seek? How does *reflection* compare with other terms, such as *inquiry, critical thinking*, and *metacognition*, which are often associated with reflective practice? One problem is that reflection has come to mean everything to everybody and, as a result, has lost much of its meaning. Rogers (2002) argues that without greater precision, the term *reflection* will be dismissed because no one will know what to look for, what to observe in practice, or ultimately what to assess.

To gain a deeper understanding of the meaning of reflection, Rogers cites Dewey (1933) and provides readers with four definitions of reflection:

- ◆ Reflection makes meaning; it moves the learner to a deeper understanding of experience and its relationship with and connections to other experiences and ideas.
- ◆ Reflection involves systemic, rigorous, and disciplined ways of thinking with roots in scientific inquiry.
- ◆ Reflection is part of a community of learners, understood in interaction with others.
- ◆ Reflection is an attitude that values the personal and intellectual growth of oneself and others (based on Rogers, 2002, p. 245).

Reflection as a meaning maker. School administrators and practitioners are sometimes accused of having experiences but missing their meanings. Administrators, by definition, engage with others in the world. They need to make sense of new events, based on a repertoire of previous experiences. Researchers indicate they "stand on the shoulders of giants" to imply that understanding is built around consensus and that learning from one source is applied in subsequent situations. Chess players gain expertise from the experiences of studying thousands of unique situations, which are then recalled and applied in new circumstances. Administrative practice is context bound, and every situation has unique qualities, which must be considered before taking action.

Experience alone is not enough; actions can become routine, or one can become cynical. The goal of reflection is to learn what to take away from one's experiences. Reflective practitioners learn from experience by connecting their individual and personal experiences with deeper and more extended considerations that are raised by knowledgeable others. "The creation of meaning out of experience is at the very heart of what it means to be human. It enables us to make sense of and attribute values to the events of our lives" (Rogers, 2002, p. 848).

Reflection as a rigorous way of thinking. Reflection is more than stream of consciousness or simply the belief that something is true; it is systematic and disciplined (Rogers, 2002). Reflection bridges one experience to the next by moving a practitioner from a state of questioning (perplexity) to a more settled state, in which the implications of experiences are not yet fully established. This process involves a certain amount of curiosity, which opens up the possibility of new learning.

Reflection as part of a community of learners. Reflection is not practiced in isolation; it occurs in a community of learners. Reflecting on experience, on what happened, requires that other people be involved in the learning. There is a need to verbalize and unpack the given circumstances of an event. What happened? What may need to be done differently in the future? Otherwise, one risks repeating the same mistakes and missing the meanings of one's experiences, instead of learning from them.

Reflection as a set of attitudes. Learning is more than a cognitive process; it involves attitudes, feelings, and emotions. Reflection encompasses attitudes about how to embrace one's experiences, wholeheartedness in embracing one's experiences, directness in scrutinizing one's own performance, open-mindedness in new ways of seeing and understanding events, and readiness to be curious and grow through reflection.

Ultimately, reflection is not an end in itself but a tool to connect everyday experiences into meaning-filled theory, which serves larger purposes of individual moral growth and societal change. Reflection is disciplined thinking and can be practiced, assessed, and perfected if learners are expected to grow from their experiences on the job and in life (based on Rogers, 2002, p. 864).

Reflection-in-Action and on-Action

How does one use the activities and assignments experienced during the internship to become a more effective principal? The simple answer is that one learns by reflecting on experiences. So far, however, the text has considered the process of reflection as an after-the-fact reconstruction of experience, *reflection-on-action*. Reflection-on-action is "the ordered, deliberate, and systematic application of logic to a problem in order to resolve it" (Russell and Munby, 1991, p. 165).

There is also a second and distinct process that Russell and Munby point to, in which practitioners adjust the ways they hear and see events in the moment and adjust accordingly. These moments are described as *reflections-in-action* and are more akin to the gestalt shifts that people experience when looking at the reversible pictures of the "old woman or young lady" or "duck or rabbit" (Gestalt Shift, 2011). The essence of reflection-in-action is in "hearing" or "seeing" things differently. For Schön (1991), this process is also called *reframing*, the application of learning to what experience teaches. New actions and new frames go hand in hand; when administrators try new things, they reframe their prior experiences. Their professional knowledge draws on experience *and* the application of theory, from rethinking and talking through one's experiences. Effective administrators move back and forth between the "knowhow" their actions demonstrate and the formal, symbolic explanations or representations of those actions. It is not one or the other; rather, the goal is to move back and forth between the two, between action and reflection, to gain a deeper understanding of administrative practices.

Learning Reflective Practice

Learning reflective practice is one of the goals of the internship. Taylor, Rudolf, and Foldy (2008) define three core stages for learning reflective practice: "1) understanding the social construction of reality, 2) recognizing one's own contribution to that construction, and 3) taking action to reshape that construction" (p. 659). Understanding the social construction of reality suggests that internal perceptions shape how people view external reality. In other words, your inner thoughts and prior experiences shape how you define situations and make inferences. Recognizing your contribution to that construction moves you away from making premature inferences and begins the more detailed, labor-intensive work of describing what is going on in a given situation. Taking action requires reframing an event in ways that alter your previous construction, in words and actions that move away from focusing on why things happen and instead provide richer and more detailed explanations for how things work in the world. It should also be clear that the three concepts are not separate and constantly intermingle with one another. You may find it useful, however, to identify them separately so you can break established patterns of seeing and acting.

In the next section (Section 3.4: Enrichment and Extended Learning Activities), you will be given examples of educational leadership policy standards along with a brief discussion of activities to apply to your own reflections. After following the steps outlined in each case scenario, your goal is to apply the three core stages of reflective practice outlined above to each of the extended learning activities.

3.4 Enrichment and Extended Learning Activities

Developing and improving leadership skills through reflection and the use of ELCC standards-based extended learning activities (ELAs) can provide a safe harbor for both the emerging and practicing leader to explore the application of theory, knowledge, skills, and dispositions to resolve a wide variety of difficult leadership dilemmas. Reading, researching, seeking expert opinion, and reflecting on the issues embedded in standards-based ELAs can provide an effective approach to learning and developing a strong leadership advantage. The following standards-based ELAs may be used in a number of ways:

- ♦ As activities in an internship plan
- ♦ As learning activities for discussions with other interns as part of a course or program
- ♦ As learning activities to remediate or expand leadership skills
- ♦ As a way to enrich or remediate—as needed—to improve performance central to certain leadership standards.

You should consult with your district or university program supervisor to decide whether to use this activity. In any case, it is highly recommended that interns complete as many of these exercises as possible.

Directions
1. Read the extended learning activities and write a brief response for each statement.
2. Indicate why you agree or disagree with each ELA.
3. After you complete your initial response to the issues contained in the ELA, discuss them with an experienced administrator.
4. Use the three core stages of reflective practice discussed in section 3.3 to inform your response.

5. Revise your responses to include learning and insights you deem to be most useful.
6. File your responses in your notebook or e-portfolio for future reflection and reference.

The Power of Vision

ELCC Standard 1.0: Candidates who complete the program are education leaders who have the knowledge and ability to promote the success of all students by facilitating the development, articulation, implementation, and stewardship of a school or district vision of learning supported by the school community.

Effective principals set high learning standards for all students. Such principals have a clear vision of what they want to accomplish, possess strong values, and have a sound set of beliefs on which to base all education policies, decisions, and actions. Effective principals know how to enlist the support of all school stakeholders to collaborate in the development of a rich, productive environment for teaching and learning. This is a critical goal to achieve because the most important factor in providing successful education programs and practices is faithful adherence to a strong set of values and beliefs together with a shared vision. There is no question that the basic philosophy, spirit, and drive of a unified administration, faculty, staff, and community have far more to do with successfully educating all children than do technology or economic resources, organizational structure, or innovation. All these factors count heavily toward success; however, they are transcended by how strongly the principal, faculty, and staff believe in basic precepts and how faithfully they carry them out.

Questions for Reflection

Does evidence show that the school leadership adheres to a clear set of values and beliefs? Does the leadership understand and use research to facilitate a positive climate for continuous, ongoing professional development for faculty and staff? Do the education leaders demonstrate a commitment to the premise that all students must be educated to achieve success in adult life? How effective is the leadership at articulating a clear vision for successful schooling and in setting high standards for learning? To what extent are faculty and staff committed to supporting high learning standards for all children and abiding by a shared vision? Do community stakeholders support high learning standards and the school vision?

After responding to the questions for reflection, you may elect to complete the following ELA to help enrich or improve your performance.

Extended Learning Activity

1. Write a vision statement for a school; share it with your site mentor and the university supervisor or with a school leadership team for evaluation and feedback.

2. Show how community and school stakeholders participated in the development of the vision.

3. Collect, interpret, and analyze school data, and draft a set of recommendations to serve as a guide for school improvement.

4. Discuss your work on the extended learning questions with your site mentor or university supervisor to gain additional insight.

5. File your responses in your notebook or e-portfolio for future reflection and reference.

Successful Leaders Focus on Vision, Quality, Equity, and Caring

ELCC Standard 1.2.a.: Candidates demonstrate the ability to articulate the components of this vision for a school and the leadership processes necessary to implement and support the vision.

A learning-centered leader knows that successfully educating children requires a sustained collaborative effort on the part of the board of education, community, faculty, staff, and administration. Ensuring that all children reach a high level of academic achievement is possible when the leadership possesses the ability to articulate, support, and sustain a vision clearly focused on quality education, equity, and caring. Successful education leaders are able to lead school and community stakeholders in the development of a clear vision, mission, and goals to guide the education of children. They lead in the development of a positive environment for teaching and learning. They create a safe harbor for the free exchange of ideas regarding what is required to successfully educate all children to live successfully as adults. Learning-centered leaders know faculty, staff, administration, and students will stay clearly focused on accomplishing the vision—as well as important education goals and high student achievement for all—only to the degree that the leadership is firmly committed to the premise that success for all is an absolute must. Learning-centered leaders produce the best results by practicing the following principles: the primary goal of successful education leadership is high academic achievement for every student. Educators achieve this lofty goal by taking genuine pride in the academic growth of all children. Leaders, educators, and children must be able to experience feelings of accomplishment and joy in their work. **Note:** Fear of failure must be expunged from the school environment. The mistaken belief that fear and sanctions represent effective motivation for either children or adults is wrong-headed thinking.

Questions for Reflection

To what extent does the leadership in the school focus on academic achievement for all students? To what extent are fear of failure and sanctions used to motivate students, faculty, staff, and administrators? Does the school use high-stakes testing to measure academic achievement? What plan is in place to accommodate the wide variety of learning needs in the school? To what extent is the leadership of the school concerned with quality, equity, and care for students, faculty, and staff? What insights, concerns, or questions do you have regarding this statement?

After responding to the questions for reflection, you may elect to complete the following ELA to help enrich or improve your performance.

Extended Learning Activity

1. Think about how to articulate a clear vision for the school that promotes high learning standards and academic achievement for all children.
2. Meet with a school administrator to discuss the kinds of skills and attributes necessary to implement, support, and sustain a clear vision of teaching and learning in the school.
3. Assess the degree to which data-based research and strategic planning focuses on addressing the educational needs of children in the school.
4. Develop a school improvement plan that employs communicating a clear vision of academic success for all children to school staff, students, parents, and the community.
5. Discuss the plan with your mentor to gain additional insight.
6. File responses in your notebook for future reflection and reference.

The Principal and Teacher Evaluation

ELCC Standard 2.0: A school administrator is an educational leader who promotes the success of students by advocating, nurturing, and sustaining a school culture and instructional program conducive to student learning and staff professional growth.

The primary purpose of teacher evaluation is to improve performance as well as to measure teacher effectiveness. Most school districts have well-developed policies, procedures, and teacher evaluation instruments for principals to employ in the process of evaluating teachers. The successful principal takes care to publish the school district's established teaching standards to inform all concerned about the criteria by which teachers will be evaluated. He or she notifies teachers prior to conducting performance evaluations so they can fully prepare to demonstrate the level of their teaching competency. During the course of an evaluation, the principal documents the teacher's instructional performance, taking care to identify both strong points and any limitations that may be observed. The principal meets with the teacher after each evaluation session to determine what the teacher thought about his or her performance as well as what the teacher might have done differently to help ensure that all students in the class achieve the learning objective(s) set forth in the lesson. Once the teacher and the principal share perspectives regarding the teacher's performance, they must collaborate to craft a teacher improvement plan, which may include mentoring, coaching, and employing the best practice relevant to the specific improvements noted.

A typical teacher improvement plan includes the following components:

◆ Fairness and ethical considerations dominate the teacher improvement plan.

◆ Areas identified as needing improvement are based on evaluation results.

◆ The teacher has an opportunity to rebut negative evaluations or request that another qualified evaluator in the school or district conduct an additional evaluation.

◆ The teacher has adequate time to bring performance up to the district's established teaching standards.

◆ The teacher has the administrative support, resources, and mentoring required to make the required improvements.

◆ The principal and the teacher schedule a subsequent teacher evaluation session to measure progress made toward meeting the district's established teaching standards.

Note: Exemplary teaching performance must be recognized and rewarded, and subpar teaching performance must be documented and corrective action must be taken to remediate inadequate performance. The successful principal knows that doing anything less is simply not acceptable.

Questions for Reflection

How strongly does the school leadership support the use of proven teaching methods, theories, and relevant curriculum to promote academic success for all students? Does the school employ a well-organized plan for teacher evaluation and ongoing professional growth and development? Are teaching evaluations based on established teaching standards? Are teaching evaluations used to improve teaching and learning? Is the evaluation of teachers fair, based on established teaching standards, and in compliance with law and district policies and procedures? What questions, concerns, or ideas do you have about the effectiveness of teaching and learning in your school? What changes would you make to enhance student achievement for all students?

After responding to the questions for reflection, you may elect to complete the following ELA to help enrich or improve your performance.

Extended Learning Activity

1. Discuss teaching evaluations with a respected school administrator; inquire about current research and best practice relevant to teaching, learning, and assessment to gain additional insight.

2. Discuss the importance of new teacher induction, mentoring, and the appropriate use of best practice to facilitate professional development.

3. Develop a written response; describe what you learned and how you can use the learning as a school leader.

4. File your response in your notebook or e-portfolio for future reflection and reference.

Cultural Bias and Standardized Tests

ELCC Standard 2.3: Candidates understand and apply research and foster a climate of continuous improvement among all members of the educational staff. Such educational leaders will commit themselves to high levels of personal and organizational performance in order to ensure implementation of this vision of learning.

Standardized tests have nothing to do with culture, economic status, or race. The claim that standardized testing has a cultural bias is off base. These tests measure what a student has learned and nothing more. The truth is this: low test scores reflect low levels of student learning. Knowledgeable educators understand that effective teaching and learning start with diagnosing what students know or do not know. Standardized tests provide educators with a useful instrument to do just that. To claim that standardized tests don't measure student learning is nonsense. Schools teach children important information they can use to develop skills and knowledge. Standardized tests measure students' level of achievement in the cognitive domain, and schools are best equipped to impart cognitive knowledge. Those who are concerned that using standardized tests will eventually lead to opening the door for test makers and the federal government to control the curriculum should know this: Washington and/or test makers will be able to control curricula in local schools only to the extent that school stakeholders permit them to do so.

Questions for Reflection

To what extent does the school use standardized testing? Do the teachers and administrators understand the tetations of using test results to inform teaching and learning decisions? Are standard tests fair to students, or are they culturally biased? Will a mandate to use standardized tests to measure the academic achievement of students lead to the government and/or the major test-publishing firms taking control of local schools? What ideas, concerns, or questions do you have regarding these questions?

Extended Learning Activity

1. Discuss the advantages and disadvantages of using standardized tests to assess student performance with a respected school administrator.
2. Explore best practices in the area of involving faculty, staff, parents, and community stakeholders in the appropriate use of standardized tests to judge academic performance.
3. Draft a list of recommendations to improve the quality of stakeholder participation in the improvement of curriculum development, delivery, assessment, and evaluation.

4. Discuss the recommendations with a mentor to gain additional insight.

5. Develop a plan to better engage parents, and form teacher focus groups about high-stakes testing and alternative methods of measuring student performance.

6. File your plan in your notebook or e-portfolio for future reflection and reference.

The Case Against High-Stakes Testing

The current school reform movement relies too heavily on a high-stakes testing approach as a way to improve the quality of education in our schools. The drive for higher levels of student achievement as evidenced by high test scores has caused state and national decision makers to ignore many of the more critical factors that must be provided to produce quality educational programs and services. Policy makers and school administrators should know that quality education comes from providing children with well-qualified teachers, a good curriculum, competent leadership, adequate supplies, books, laboratories, and other necessary school facilities. They must also understand this reality: quality education has never come from testing nor will it ever. One need to look no further than the current school reform movement to see the failure associated with trying to produce better student achievement by using high-stakes testing to judge the quality of education.

Learning-centered leaders know that teachers, administrators, staff, and students must be allowed to succeed in their respective roles by demonstrating more concern for the individual dignity of all. Emphasis must be placed on teaching and learning. Students must have the resources and time to master the knowledge, skills, and dispositions required to achieve academic success. Testing must be relegated to its only legitimate use: discovering what students know and what they need to learn to achieve academic competency. When this goal is reached, standardized test scores that state and national policy makers demand might be achieved. Continued misuse of high-stakes testing will most certainly render that outcome impossible. And for good reasons: state and federal policy makers have a shortsighted view of what constitutes a quality education. They lack the necessary understanding and knowledge of the complex process of educating children. They want excellence in education, but they don't have a clue about what constitutes a quality education. Unfortunately, too many of them believe that a fear of failure will motivate educators, parents, and students to do a better job. Nothing could be further from the truth. Fear of failure and severe sanctions over the long term can serve only to interfere with, impede, and ultimately arrest learning.

Questions for Reflection

How does the school leadership use high-stakes tests to evaluate the success of students? To what extent are such tests used to measure the performance of the administration, faculty, staff, and school? How does high-stakes testing affect the curriculum? How much time do teachers and students spend preparing for testing? What do teachers, parents, and students think about the value of high-stakes testing? What insights, concerns, or questions do you have regarding these questions?

Extended Learning Activity

1. Review the school curriculum and assessment plan, and discuss the plan with your mentor to gain additional insight.
2. Evaluate the curriculum goals and learning objectives, and determine the extent to which the goals and objectives are directly relevant to the evaluation and assessment tools used measure student performance.
3. Analyze student achievement in the school, compare and contrast academic achievement among various groups within the student population, and identify any area of concerns that may need to be addressed.
4. Draft a list of recommendations to improve the use of student assessments to measure academic performance.
5. Discuss your findings and recommendations with a respected mentor to gain additional information and perspective.
6. File the response in your notebook or e-portfolio for future reflection and reference.

A Management Responsibility: Supervision of Programs and Personnel

Standard 3.0: Candidates who complete the program are educational leaders who have the knowledge and ability to promote the success of all students by managing the organization, operations, and resources in a way that promotes a safe, efficient, and effective learning environment.

Principals have a responsibility to manage school programs and personnel in ways to ensure that faculty, staff, and students have a safe, orderly environment. Principals must hold themselves and others strictly accountable to perform professional duties and responsibilities, without fail. One way to help achieve this goal is to make sure that all concerned with the education of students understand the nature of their professional responsibilities and are diligent in the execution of those duties. Simply put: when principals, teachers, or other educators fail to effectively perform assigned duties, they are negligent. Failure to supervise students may be intentional or unintentional depending on the nature of the ineffective performance. Failure to supervise constitutes neglect of duty, which is commonly defined as a failure to carry out professional obligations and responsibilities in connection with classroom or other school sponsored activities.

Successful principals know that neglect of duty is not measured against a standard of perfection but rather against a standard required of others performing the same or similar duties. They also know that educators who do not meet this standard are derelict in their duty to protect and are therefore subject to disciplinary action up to and including litigation, termination, and loss of professional certification.

Questions for Reflection

How effective is the school leadership regarding the promotion and support of a safe, orderly learning environment? Do the students, faculty, and staff feel safe and secure in the school? What is the community perception of school safety, security, and the overall care and supervision of students? What would you do to improve conditions in the school to ensure that all concerned can enjoy a school environment conducive to success for all students? What questions and/or concerns do you have about the culture and climate in your school and community?

Extended Learning Activity

1. Discuss the issue of supervising students with a respected school administrator to gain additional insight.
2. Meet with teachers, parents, and a community group to discuss their perceptions or opinions about the issue.
3. Formulate a list of recommendations to improve supervision, and identify strategies to address any negative opinions and perceptions.
4. Develop a written response; describe what you learned and how you can use the learning as a school leader.
5. To enhance your performance as a school leader in this area, be sure that your response is clear and in sufficient depth to demonstrate a full understanding of the issues.
6. File your response in your notebook or e-portfolio for future reflection and reference.

Managing School Employee Misconduct

Historically, the problem of teacher conduct, including molestation, was handled in a variety of ways. Some administrators simply ignored or dismissed any complaints. Others allowed the offending party to move on to another school, often with a good recommendation regarding his or her teaching ability. These administrators used such methods to avoid embarrassment, which always accompanies charges of child molestation. To be sure, some administrators moved to terminate school employees, but termination was rare. The "it's best not to air dirty laundry in public" approach was often used because it meant not having to deal with the problem. Some administrators attempt to justify this approach because of a mistaken belief that molestation charges are hard to prove without a complete investigation. They also mistakenly believe that an investigation and any subsequent litigation that results will be more hostile toward the child than toward the adult involved. The adult will be believed rather than the child. The child's parents will not want their child exposed to further harm from an investigation and/or legal action, or worse, they won't want to damage the career of an educator. Today, there are very serious consequences for those who fail to follow proper procedures regarding the duty to report all suspected incidents of child abuse, including molestation. Many administrators have faced the problem of having to deal with charges of molestation. If they have yet to experience the problem, they probably know of a colleague who has. The bottom line is this: charges of molestation are serious and must be handled in accordance with established school board policy and the law.

Questions for Reflection

What does board policy stipulate regarding ways in which charges of molestation must be handled? What steps has the school administrator taken to ensure that all concerned understand and abide by policies and laws governing the reporting of child molestation? Has legal counsel reviewed school policies to ensure that they comply with state law? What insights, concerns, or questions do you have regarding these questions?

Extended Learning Activity

1. Review board policy relevant to employee misconduct to determine how to manage unprofessional behavior.
2. Discuss the issue with an experienced school administrator to better understand the scope and magnitude of employee misconduct and the ways in which such behavior adversely impacts the teaching and learning climate of the school.
3. Discuss the legal requirements relevant to employee misconduct, including harassment and molestation, with your mentor to gain additional information and insight on the issue.
4. Explore best practices and policies that can be employed to manage school operations, programs, and personnel to ensure a safe, orderly school environment for all concerned.
5. Develop a management plan to guide in the supervision and evaluation of programs, personnel, and practices to help ensure that professional conduct is central to the management and operations of the school.
6. File the plan in your notebook or e-portfolio for future reflection and reference.

Changing Role of Schools: Success for All Children

Standard 4.0: Candidates who complete the program are educational leaders who have the knowledge and ability to promote the success of all students by collaborating with families and other community members, responding to diverse community interests and needs, and mobilizing community resources.

Historically, a primary purpose of schooling in the United States was to act as a "gatekeeper" or—put another way—to sort out the population. The gatekeeper role served as a cost-effective way to prepare a select group of students to qualify for admission to colleges and universities. Other students were targeted to participate in technical/vocational training programs, and the remaining students were expected to transition directly from school to the workplace. The rationale for using schools as gatekeepers was based on the thinking that a limited number of highly educated people were needed to fill professional roles and other high-level occupations. The problem is that the transition toward globalization has resulted in a drastic change in societal needs and conditions. Powerful new economic forces and workplace needs now demand a more highly skilled workforce. Policy makers and enlightened education leaders recognized the globalization movement during the early part of the last decade and immediately began to advocate for a significant change in the role of schooling in this country.

State and national leaders determined that schools needed to discard the gatekeeper role and help all students realize their potential. Make no mistake: a tremendous amount of money has been spent on a variety of school reform initiatives during the last decade. Though some progress has been made, the educational needs of too many children are simply not being addressed. "Broken promises and forgotten children" perhaps best describes the plight of an ever-increasing number of students in schools today. Children born into unhealthful environments and raised on the painful edge of poverty and/or within the walls of troubled homes have little or no hope for a better future, unless schools take certain steps to better educate them. Successful leaders know that academic programs must accommodate the learning needs of all children, especially the disadvantaged. There is no question that schools, teachers, and school administrators must be held accountable for the academic success of all children, with no excuses and no exceptions.

Questions for Reflection

What are the most serious obstacles to ensuring academic success for at-risk children in the school? Has the school identified students who might be at risk academically? What specific steps has the school taken to support teachers and administrators in their effort to ensure that all students (including at-risk children) succeed academically? Do school leaders hold themselves, faculty, and staff accountable for ensuring that all children achieve academic success? What insights, concerns, or questions do you have regarding these questions?

After responding to the questions for reflection, you may elect to complete the following ELA to help enrich or improve your performance.

Extended Learning Activity

1. Assess and evaluate the school's teaching and learning culture and climate.
2. Discuss your findings with faculty and school leaders to gain additional insight.

3. Identify educational programs, practices, and services that effectively address the critical components of social justice, diversity, language, special needs, gender, and the ethnic and socioeconomic needs of children in the school and community.

4. Develop a proposed school improvement plan designed to help facilitate academic success for all children attending the school.

5. Discuss your work on the extended learning questions with your site mentor or university supervisor to gain additional insight.

6. File your responses in your notebook or e-portfolio for future reflection and reference.

The Power of Parent Involvement

ELCC Standard 4.0: Collaborate with families and other community members responding to diverse community interests and needs and mobilizing community resources.

Studies regarding student success in school continue to validate the importance of parental involvement and community support in the education of children. Research demonstrates that academic achievement correlates more closely with parent involvement and community support than with economic status, race, or peer pressure. Parental involvement also proves to be beneficial to all ethnic groups. Active participation by either fathers or mothers has been found to benefit boys and girls equally. Research shows that children do better in school when a parent or guardian is involved. Simply put, children whose parents or guardians are involved in their education experience a powerful academic benefit. Further, less educated parents who actively participate in the education of their children appear to exert a greater influence on the academic success of their children than do their more educated counterparts. Significantly, high-risk students may benefit most from marshaling community engagement and parental involvement in their education. The bottom line: research findings on parental involvement and academic achievement make getting parents involved in the education of their children a top priority for school leaders.

Questions for Reflection

Does the school have a plan to involve parents in the education of their children? What evidence exists to validate the extent of parental involvement? Does the school's mission clearly address parent involvement in children's education? What ideas, concerns, or questions do you have regarding these questions?

Extended Learning

1. Review the school improvement plan, and identify ways in which the community, parents, and other resources are organized to help promote the academic success of all students.

2. Discuss the issue of community and parent involvement in the school with a respected school administrator to gain additional insight.

3. Organize a group of school and community stakeholders to help identify ways in which they might increase their participation to help support a high level of academic achievement for all students in the school.

4. Develop a plan to help engage families and the community in the education of students.

5. Share the plan with a respected school leader to obtain feedback, and revise as may be indicated.

6. File your responses in your notebook or e-portfolio for future reflection and reference.

Building Public Support

ELCC Standard 5.0: Candidates who complete the program are educational leaders who have the knowledge and ability to promote the success of all students by acting with integrity, fairly, and in an ethical manner.

Power used in unethical ways always does damage to the climate for teaching and learning in schools. Administrators should periodically evaluate their use of power to ensure that the power associated with a given position is not misused. This involves asking some hard questions. An administrator should determine whether he or she has taken any action to influence the outcome of a decision to benefit a close friend, family member, or special interest group. The administrator should also ask whether he or she has attempted to change the outcome of a disciplinary decision or assignment of a grade or influence the purchase of school supplies. These are just a few examples of the manner in which administrative power is most often misused. Unethical use of power results in loss of community support, public trust, and, in some cases, criminal charges against the administrator. Perhaps even worse, the misuse of power always has a negative effect on students and their quality of education. In contrast, using administrative power in ethical ways results in building trust and support for schools and educators; most important, the ethical use of power forms the foundation on which a strong climate for teaching and learning can be constructed.

Questions for Reflection

How would I react if I witnessed an administrator using power in unethical ways? What steps should an administrator take to ensure that power is used only in ethical ways? What role should school board policy play in protecting against the misuse of power in the school? What insights, concerns, or questions do you have regarding these questions?

Extended Learning Activity

1. Review board policy governing ethical behavior in the school.

2. With an experienced administrator, discuss the critical role ethics have in the development and support of a healthy climate for teaching and learning.
3. Observe the behavior and actions of school leaders to identify occasions when behavior serves to promote trust, confidence, and support for administrative decisions and actions. Identify the ones that may have a negative impact on the school climate.
4. Develop a position statement on the importance of values and ethics and their relationship to leadership success.
5. File your statement in your notebook or e-portfolio for future reflection and reference.

The Principal and Ethical Behavior

When thinking about the importance of a person who has been set apart to accomplish a public purpose, such as a principal, a teacher, a doctor, an accountant, a police officer, etc., it is important to keep in mind that good ethical behavior is a leadership must. In fact, most people don't look kindly on the exceptions. Perhaps this is because we depend on others to abide by rules of good ethical behavior just as they depend on us. Most people do not violate rules of good behavior or ignore laws or public policy set forth to help ensure that everyone may enjoy a safe, orderly society. Though some may reserve the right to grouse about rules, policy, or the law, few people knowingly seek to evade their responsibilities. People trust. They trust their neighbor, accountant, banker, attorney, and the airline pilot. Experience may make people cautious concerning human failure and those exceptions when their trust might have been shaken. But that is the point: these are exceptions.

People who take on the role of school leadership become something more than themselves. They carry the dreams and the hopes people have for their children. This is worth keeping in mind for people who prepare and work toward providing effective leadership in their schools, communities, and the nation. The bottom line is this: school principals must be fully committed to setting and demonstrating high standards of ethical behavior in their schools and communities.

Questions for Reflection

How effective is the school leadership with regard to setting and abiding by high standards of ethical behavior for all concerned? What could you do to help ensure that others view you as a model for good ethical behavior? What questions, concerns, or ideas do you have regarding leadership and ethics?

Extended Learning Activity

1. Reflect on the relationships among communications, ethics, and effective leadership.
2. Discuss the topic with a respected school leader to gain additional insight.

3. Develop a written response; describe what you learned and how you can use the learning as a school leader.
4. File your response in your notebook or e-portfolio for future reflection and reference.

After completing the steps above, attend a community meeting, a faculty meeting, and at least one meeting of the school's governing board and answer the questions listed below.

♦ During the meetings, did the leaders speak clearly and distinctly so the audience could follow discussions easily?
♦ Did the leadership demonstrate respect for all concerned?
♦ Did the leadership limit comments to the items listed on the meeting agenda?
♦ Did the leadership use data rather than personal beliefs or opinions to help formulate decisions and actions?
♦ Did the leadership take care to decide matters according to established policy and regulations?
♦ Did the leaders communicate with one another in a logical, well-organized manner?
♦ Did the leaders model ethics, enhance trust, and show respect for the organization?

The Power of Perception

ELCC Standard 6.2: Candidates demonstrate the ability to communicate with members of a school community concerning trends, issues, and potential changes in the environment in which the school operates, including maintenance of an ongoing dialogue with representatives of diverse community groups.

With increasing frequency, administrators and teachers hear complaints about how poorly schools of today perform as compared to the schools of old. "In my day, schools had superior academic standards." "Students were better behaved, and student achievement was far higher than is the case with the schools of today." Further, a growing number of citizens openly claim that the schools of yesterday produced far better results at a fraction of the cost than do the schools of today. To support this position, school critics point to a growing number of national reports showing that literacy rates are rapidly declining, drug abuse is on the increase, dropout rates are rising at an alarming rate, and educators and schools are out of touch with the needs of society. The main point is this: left unchanged, perceptions that schools are failing to effectively educate our children erode community confidence, which leads to a loss of support.

One way to create a positive perception of schools is to organize a task force of educators and community stakeholders. Members of the task force can then collaborate on the development of a brand or slogan that matches the image the school wants to project. The process begins with selecting key words that help create a positive picture of the school. Leaders in business and industry understand that words can have a strong impact on perceptions and serve as a rallying point to boost support for an organization. The effective principal understands this reality and plans accordingly to engender public trust and confidence in the school.

Questions for Reflection

Is there a fundamental difference between the schools of yesterday and today? Do the school administrators and teachers carefully identify the specific strengths of the school's academic programs and services? Do administrators and teachers build on those strengths in ways that will facilitate higher levels of academic and social success for all students? Does the school leadership maintain an ongoing dialogue with school and community stakeholders? What ideas, concerns, or questions do you have regarding these questions?

Once you complete the questions for reflection, you may elect to respond to the following ELA to help enrich or improve your performance.

Extended Learning Activity

1. What do people in the community think of the school's quality of education?
2. Review and evaluate the school improvement plan to determine how students, parents, and other community stakeholders are involved in the process of influencing and supporting the adoption of sound education policy and law.
3. Develop recommendations and strategies that you think will help facilitate policies that benefit students and their families.
4. Review education policy in your school to identify ways in which those policies might be improved to better promote the kinds of academic programs and services that will help ensure that all students are well educated.
5. Review the school public information plan, and make recommendations for improving relations with the media.
6. Identify the steps you would take to respond to attacks the quality of the school.
7. Discuss the issue with your mentor to gain feedback and additional insight, and revise your responses as needed.
8. File your responses in your notebook or e-portfolio for future reflection and reference.

3.5 Technology and Leadership

Why is it more important than ever that prospective school administrators become knowledgeable about the use of technology in schools? First, today's students are digital natives (Prensky, 2001). Various forms of technology have been an integral part of their lives since birth, and they expect regular technology accessibility during instruction. School leaders need to be aware of the ways technology can effectively contribute to higher student achievement and support continued school-improvement initiatives.

Second, school administrators need to become familiar with the ways emerging, interactive technologies can facilitate efficiency, collaboration, and personalization for learning and communication. Using a variety of Internet-based resources, mobile devices, electronic archiving, and online learning communities promotes a green learning environment and reduces time and funds needed to maintain traditional systems.

Last, interns need to learn about the ethical and social aspects of technology use. This includes familiarization with district and federal policies related to the student—remember, most students are minors—and staff use of various forms of technologies, such as the Internet, databases, file sharing, e-mail, and digital archiving.

Technology Today and Tomorrow

Many digital-age tools available for teaching and learning in today's schools are free and easily obtained. Virtual worlds, online learning, and Web 2.0 tools invade the real world (Lemke and Coughlin, 2009). School administrators take the lead for using Web 2.0 applications for learning. Building a vision for using new tools to support educational change is the responsibility of all school administrators. Research shows that students who use technology tools every day achieve at higher levels. Learning to use the new social-media learning tools empowers the campus and the district leader to assist others in understanding the need and support for the anytime, anywhere learning environment.

> The term Web 2.0 refers to Web applications that make participating in information sharing, user-centered design, and collaboration on the World Wide Web much easier than in the past. A Web 2.0 site encourages users to create online interactions and collaborate with one another in a social media conversation as originators of user-generated content in an online community, in contrast to websites where users are limited to the passive reading of content that was created for them. Examples of Web 2.0 include social networking sites, blogs, wikis, video sharing sites, and Web applications. (Retrieved from http://en.wikipedia.org/wiki/Web_2.0).

Technology today is more than the word processing and spreadsheets of the past, although those productivity tools continue to be important. As predicted by Solomon and Schrum (2010), Web 2.0 resources are reaching a critical mass and new tools are easier to use, more transparent, and a more necessary part of school. Cloud computing is a recognized resource on most campuses today. Working in the cloud simply means that information is stored on the Internet and can be accessed and used by the owner from anywhere. The information no longer resides only on the personal computer at home or at school. This shift in visionary technology offers shared resources, software, and information on demand. Web 2.0 tools also offer instructional social media and interactive paths for teaching and learning.

Students create and submit outcomes-based reflective portfolios. Students learn how to use the tools for learning. Outside of school, students text and use instant messaging while listening to music and browsing the Web. According to the Kaiser Family Foundation Report 7593 (as cited by Lemke and Coughlin, 2009), "Most students do not know how to use the tools instructionally to become intelligent learners, creative producers, and effective communicators." School leaders are responsible for using the tools and teaching children how to become informed consumers.

Students and teachers should focus on finding, synthesizing, and analyzing information and using it to create knowledge collaboratively and communicating the results—all online as technology shifts to Web-based operations in cloud computing. Solomon and Schrum (2010) also predict that district operations will move to the cloud. The annual Horizon Report (Johnson, Smith, et al., 2011) cited four major trends:

1. The abundance of resources and relationships made easily accessible via the Internet is increasingly challenging us to revisit our roles as educators in sense making, coaching, and credentialing.
2. People expect to be able to work, learn, and study whenever and wherever they want.
3. The world of work is increasingly collaborative, giving rise to reflection about the way student projects are structured.
4. The technologies we use are increasingly cloud-based, and our notions of IT support are decentralized. (Read the report at www.nmc.org/pdf/2011-Horizon-Report-K12.)

What Do Prospective School Administrators Need to Know About Technology?

This may be the first time in the American public school experience when many students are more knowledgeable and proficient in a field (technology) than their teachers. This condition gives rise to the concept promoted over many years of including student input in the choice of learning activities and modalities. In short, educators can try to compete with tech savvy students or utilize their knowledge and skill for school improvement. Technology use is part of American culture, and new school leaders should do the following:

♦ Keep abreast of emerging technologies and their impact on school improvement.

- Utilize school, district, and grant resources to maintain updated technology resources. Elicit assistance from school and community stakeholders.
- Become very familiar with the ethical and social aspects of technology use. This component includes a full understanding of district and federal policies related to the use and abuse of various forms of technology, such as the Internet, databases, file sharing, e-mail, and digital archiving, by minors and staff.
- Understand that technologies should be interoperable rather than isolated.
- Provide ongoing support and resources for faculty and staff professional development related to technology applications and integration into the curriculum.
- Recognize that online learning has become a critical resource and learning medium for all ages.
- Understand that online professional learning communities and personalized learning plans are becoming the norm in 21st-century home and work environments.

3.6 Journal

"The brain does its best reflective work when provided with the time, place, and tools for the deliberate exercise of reasoning skills" (Dickmann and Stanford-Blair, 2002, p. 206). The benefits of keeping a journal have been identified as expanding awareness, understanding, and insights; making connections between theory and practice; and generating new hypotheses for action (Taggart & Wilson, 1998). Interns are strongly urged to keep journals.

Journaling helps the emerging leader focus on essential leadership skills, knowledge, and needed disposition. Journaling also provides an opportunity for interns to reflect on the results of their efforts. Time and thought used in journal writing reinforce learning and help emerging leaders to truly begin reflection prior to, during, and after action. Interns often keep journal entries in a separate file on the computer; others prefer handwritten formats. The type of journal an intern keeps is a personal choice. You may find journal entries helpful in compiling your final report.

Typical journal formats include the following:

- Daily (five to ten minutes)—Many interns try journaling for two to three weeks and reflect on patterns found following this period.
- Weekly (30 to 45 minutes)—Many try journaling for one month or an entire semester or year and reflect on patterns monthly.
- Intermittent—Many make journal entries following significant insights, feelings, and/or experiences.

♦ Projects—Many keep a journal while leading major projects and reflecting on the leadership experience and results.

The following questions may help you write your reflective entries:

♦ What belief, experience, or disposition caused a particular judgment?
♦ Reflecting on the day, did any of your actions/experiences leave you with nagging doubts? If so, why?
♦ How did you arrive at a decision? Did you consider other alternatives? Why was your choice the best one?
♦ Did you react differently to students, peers, or supervisors? If so, why?
♦ Did you notice any personal problems or experiences, e.g., stress, frustration, fatigue, happiness, warm relationships, etc.? What do you believe was the cause?
♦ Did you observe any changes in knowledge, skill, or disposition?
♦ How were your actions conducive to increased learning, school improvement, and/or development of self and others?
♦ How did your experience provide progress on mastery of state and/or national standards?

3.7 Log

The intern must meet with the supervisor and agree on the method of documenting the internship experience. Typically, a log should cite date, time (rounded to the half-hour), a brief statement describing the activity, and the state or national standard met. An example:

Date	Time	Description of Activity	Standard
9/05/12	1.0 hour	Conducted a classroom observation of Ms. Smith's history teaching.	2.1c

Many internship programs require a reflective statement following each log entry. The advantage to this is that interns must reflect immediately. Other programs separate the journal and summative log by requiring a more in-depth reflective journal entry. An intern should meet with his or her supervisor and collaboratively decide which method best meets the needs of the intern and the program.

3.8 Monitoring/Formative Evaluation

Plans always have to be changed. Typically, these changes occur because of the following:

+ Unexpected events
+ New opportunities
+ Suggestions/recommendations from mentors and/or interviewees
+ New perspectives gained from experience and reflection
+ Results of periodic formative evaluations.

Any or all of the above can arise and cause an intern to adjust, add, and/or delete planned activities. The intern should determine and schedule periodic assessment of the progress and plan. Formative evaluation should be completed monthly or more often, if needed. This should be a combination of self-evaluation and supervisor observation. It is recommended that after self-evaluation on progress and accomplishments, the intern meet with his or her supervisor and collaboratively discuss the quality and quantity of intern activities undertaken thus far and timelines for completing the remainder of the planned activities. The discussion should include gains in knowledge, skill, and disposition and effects on learning and school improvement.

The formative evaluations should note any changes to the plan and include brief explanations of the circumstances and rationales for changes. A summary of the formative evaluations, noting progress and changes, will be presented at the final internship report.

Summative Evaluation

4.1 Summary and Evaluation of Experience

The intern is required to complete a summary and an evaluation of experience for *each* of the 38 leadership areas. One summary and evaluation for each area is required, regardless of the amount of time or number of activities accomplished in the particular leadership area. The summary and evaluation of experience should be brief (one page or less) and include the following:

♦ Brief description of activity or activities in the area
♦ Significant knowledge attained, skill developed, and/or disposition improved
♦ Additional knowledge, skill development, and/or change in disposition needed
♦ Recommendations for school improvement in this area
♦ Personal beliefs/values concerning this area and motivation to lead in this area

4.2 Reflection on Action

The intern's goal is to observe more and have a greater range of models to draw from as he or she reflects on personal actions and the actions of others. Interns summarize and provide highlights of their experiences with reflective practice (see Section 3.3). They should also discuss the following in an overall *reflection on practice*:

♦ What models/concepts/theories were effective or not effective?
♦ What deep-seated beliefs guided your actions and experience?
♦ How did the history/traditions/culture of the school/district affect your actions?
♦ How did your emotional state/moods affect your actions and experience?
♦ How did the availability or lack of resources affect your actions?
♦ How did the on-the-job experience change your beliefs and actions?

4.3 Increased Learning and School Improvement: Results and Recommendations

Interns review all aspects of their internships and compile a prioritized list of all *results* of increased learning and school improvement. Interns should also submit a second prioritized list of *recommendations* to increase learning and school improvement. The results and recommendations lists are presented and submitted as part of the internship final report.

4.4 Portfolio Development

A portfolio is a compilation of relevant evidence of knowledge, skill, and disposition. It may include degrees and certificates but is primarily the best samples of your professional work and accomplishments. A professional portfolio should not be a scrapbook of training certificates, school papers, or notes from students.

Secondary principal interns should review their own state standards, the Educational Leadership Policy Standards: ISLLC 2008, and NASSP standards. Elementary principal interns should review state standards, the Educational Leadership Policy Standards: ISLLC 2008, and NAESP standards. It is recommended that interns use these as portfolio sections and provide evidence that they meet or are progressing in meeting these standards.

At this point in leadership development, it is understood that interns may not have documentation or evidence of meeting all the standards. This is the beginning of the portfolio, however, and should guide the planning of future professional development.

4.5 Vita Update

Interns should update their vitae to include relevant accomplishments from their internships. This may be included in the leadership section of the vita for those not currently holding an administrative position. For experienced administrators, this is typically placed under the professional development category or administrative experience category. Guidelines for developing the vita are listed in Appendix A.1. A copy of the updated vita should be presented at the final internship report.

4.6 Letter of Application

The letter of application should focus on the specific career goal of the intern. For example, if the intern wants the position of assistant superintendent for curriculum, the letter of application should be written for that position. If the intern would like an assistant principal position prior to applying for a principalship, the letter should be written for that position. Guidelines for the letter of application are listed in Appendix A.2. The letter of application should be presented at the final internship report.

4.7 Future Professional Development Plan

The intern must prepare and submit a three-year professional development plan based on his or her internship experience. This plan should discuss the following:

♦ Progress toward meeting the Educational Leadership Policy Standards: ISLLC 2008
♦ Successes and failures in the intern experience
♦ Reflections in and on action
♦ Self, peer, and superior evaluations
♦ Position and leadership goals

Typically, a professional development plan focuses on the priorities or greatest needs of the leader. The plan must be clear and manageable and include a means of evaluation.

A clear plan lists specific objectives. It should cite actions to take, as opposed to a vague or general intent to improve in a particular area. This could include specific courses, workshops, books, work with a mentor, or a host of other experiences. The intern must research available resources to meet his or her objectives. Objectives may include developing skills, reevaluating dispositions, or attaining new knowledge.

A manageable plan includes actions that can be accomplished in a reasonable amount of time. Typically, three to five objectives are included in a three-year plan. This allows the intern time to use or practice the new knowledge, disposition, or skill. A timeline for each objective must be included.

The plan must cite the criteria used to judge whether the objective was met. Ideally, this would be an artifact or other evidence that could be included in the portfolio. The professional development plan is submitted at the final internship report.

4.8 Internship Report

In this final activity, the intern will prepare and present an overall report. Typically, the intern presents to his or her supervisors, either as part of many reports by others or individually. The report must be a professional presentation, similar to reporting to the school board. Documentation should include the items listed below. Following each item is the section in the text where the item is found.

♦ Summary of individual skill assessment (1.2)
♦ Summary of disposition assessment/other assessments and evaluations (1.3, 1.4)
♦ Position and leadership goals (1.5)
♦ Summary of school/district goals and/or improvement plan (1.6)
♦ Summary and evaluation of experience (4.1)

- Summary of local project(s) (2.4)
- Summary of reflective practice (4.2)
- School improvement lists (4.3)
- Updated vita (4.5)
- Portfolio (4.4)
- Letter of application (4.6)
- Activities notebook or e-portfolio (2.6)
- Networking list (2.5)
- Professional resources and affiliations (2.1, #37)
- Three-year professional development plan (4.7)
- Journal (3.6)
- Log (3.7)

The intern should use overheads or PowerPoint to show highlights of the overall experience. The length of the report should be agreed upon with supervisors prior to the presentation.

Appendix A.1 Sample Vita and Guidelines

George Washington

1508 West 14th Street, Mount Vernon, AZ 50555

(W) (303) 555-7837; (H) (303) 555-9069; gwash@used.org

Education/Certification

M.Ed.—Education Leadership, Northern Arizona University, Flagstaff, AZ, 2004

BA—English, Carleton College, Northfield, MN, 1993

Principal Certificate—Arizona (in progress)

Teacher Certificate—7–12 English: Arizona and Minnesota

ESL Education—K–12 Endorsement, Arizona and Minnesota

Administrative and Leadership Experience

Assistant Principal, Martha High School, Mount Vernon Union High School District, Vernon, AZ, 2000–present.

- Administered campus activities including over fifty school clubs, school facility use, and school ceremonies.

- Expanded the student recognition program designed to reward and promote student attendance, academic achievement, and responsible actions on campus.

- Evaluated and provided guidance for a variety of teachers throughout the school using the district's evaluation instrument and informal observations and conferences.

English Department Chairperson, Martha High School, Mount Vernon, AZ, 1999–2000.

- Designed a department-based professional literacy library and conference center to help teachers better their pedagogical skills.

- Implemented an English department collaborative teaching plan that promoted positive teacher communication regarding units and lessons, methodology, classroom management, and student achievement.

- Planned and presented various English department in-services designed to improve classroom instruction, time management, and grant writing.

- Evaluated all English teachers using the district's evaluation instrument and informal observations while carefully monitoring the progress of new and inexperienced teachers.

North Central Accreditation Writing Goal Chairman, Martha High School, Mount Vernon, AZ, 1999–present.

- Designed and implemented an in-service program for teachers in all subject areas to ensure successful writing instruction across the curriculum.

- Presented instructional methodology to assist all staff members in teaching and using the six-trait writing rubric, creating quality writing prompts, and teaching paragraph and essay organization.

Learning 24/7 Leadership Team Member, Martha High School, Mount Vernon, AZ, 2000–present.
- Advised and designed a school-wide plan to assure students' success in the classroom, on standardized tests, and in life.
- Aligned school curricula; incorporated test-taking skills into the curriculum; created a strong school-wide emphasis on basic reading, writing, and math skills in every class; and incorporated critical-thinking skills across the curriculum.
- Evaluated the specific instructional needs of students and teachers by meticulously surveying and analyzing student test data, grades, and district assessments.

Head Basketball Coach, Martha High School, Mount Vernon, AZ, 1995–2000.
- Incorporated a successful parent booster club that raised funds to support the basketball program.

Teaching Experience
High School English Teacher—Martha High School, Mt. Vernon, AZ, 1994–2000.
- Integrated a variety of teaching methods and instructional strategies to generate student interest.
- Tracked and evaluated student progress in class by using a combination of student work samples and evaluations.
- Maintained positive relationships with students and parents while holding students to a high standard of acceptable class work.

Upward Bound English Teacher—Normandale Upward Bound Program, Normandale Community College, Richfield, MN, 1994.
- Designed a writing workshop for students involved to create, edit, and revise their own work in a summer writing portfolio.
- Published a variety of works from every student's summer writing portfolio in a book distributed to all students and parents at the end of the summer.

Coaching Experience
Head Basketball Coach, Martha High School, Mount Vernon, AZ, 1995–2000.
- Created a successful basketball program that won at least 19 games in each of the last three seasons while maintaining a team grade point average greater than 3.2.

Additional Training/Professional Development
"Cutting Edge Grant Writing," Otter Creek Institute, Phoenix, AZ, May 2000.
"Increasing Student Achievement," National School Conference Institute, Phoenix, AZ, March 2000.

Presentations
Washington, G. (2000, September). *Improving Student Writing*. Presentation at the Inter-District Articulation Program, Mount Vernon, AZ.

Washington, G. (2000, September). *Incorporating Writing in all Classrooms.* Presentation at the Martha High School Faculty In-service, Mount Vernon, AZ.

Washington, G. (2000, August). *NCA Writing Goal and the Six-Trait Writing Rubric.* Presentation at the Martha High School In-service Program, Mount Vernon, AZ.

Professional Affiliations

Association for Supervision and Curriculum Development, 1999–present

National Association of Secondary School Principals, 2000–present

Arizona Professional Educators, 2000–present

References

References will be included on the following page, if requested.

Guidelines for Developing the Vita

Overall Guidelines

- Develop well-defined categories and sections in the appropriate order.
- Be neat and conservative; use white or beige paper, and leave plenty of space around type.
- Be accurate and ethical.
- Emphasize accomplishments.
- Include the results of accomplishments, if any; include supporting evidence in your portfolio.
- Omit information not relevant to your professional life.
- Use a clear, readable font; choose size 12 for most fonts.
- Maintain grammatical correctness; for example, make verb tenses consistent, use parallel construction, make sure nouns and verbs and nouns and pronouns agree in number.
- Use several pages—a vita is longer than a one-page business résumé.

Preferred Order of Categories

Choose the categories that are most accurate, ethical, and appropriate. Other categories or combinations of these and others for unique individuals and/ or experiences may be used.

- Heading
- Education/Certification
- Administrative, supervisory, and/or leadership experience
- Teaching experience
- Coaching experience (if applicable)
- Related experience (if applicable)
- Other experience (if applicable)
- Professional development
- Publications and/or presentations and/or grants (if applicable)
- Curriculum experience (if applicable)
- Professional affiliations
- Honors and/or awards (if applicable)
- Community involvement/service
- Professional references
- Reference page

Heading Guidelines

- Make heading three lines in length.
- Use your full legal name, and make it **stand out**.
- Provide complete address, phone number(s) with area codes, and e-mail address.

Education/Certification Category Guidelines

+ Highlight degree.
+ Follow degree with area of degree, institution name, city, state, and year awarded.
+ List major and/or minor, if appropriate and useful.
+ Do not include address of institution.
+ Note any significant amount of course hours that did not lead to a degree.
+ Insert space to separate certificates from degrees.
+ Cite certificates exactly as written on certificates and include the state.
+ List administrative certificate(s) first.
+ Place any endorsements after teaching certificates.
+ Include current certification or certification being sought. For any certification being sought, use either (In Progress) or (Expected completion date, month and year) afterward.

Administrative and/or Leadership Category Guidelines

+ Use the administrative experience category only if you were certified and served in an administrative position. It is unethical to invent a title, for example, assistant principal, if you only assisted the principal.
+ Use the supervisory experience category only if you were certified and supervised adults.
+ Use the leadership experience category for all other leadership roles, for example, department or grade-level chair, committee chair, site-council member, etc.
+ Categories are combinable; for example, use supervisory/leadership experience if you have experience in both.
+ List title first, then school, city, state, and date(s).
+ Use bullets and relevant past tense verbs for all accomplishments, for example, wrote, implemented, supervised, etc.
+ List any results of accomplishment, if known and appropriate.
+ Use two to six bullets under each title.

Teaching Experience Category Guidelines

+ Capitalize and list title first, then organization or school, city, state, and date(s).
+ Use bullets and relevant past tense verbs, for example, *wrote, implemented, supervised*, etc.
+ List any results of accomplishments, if known.
+ Use two to six bullets, typically more if the accomplishments are very recent or span a significant number of years, in the following format:
  • Title, organization or school, city, state, date(s)
  • Past tense verb + accomplishment + results

- Past tense verb + accomplishment + results
- Past tense verb + accomplishment
- Past tense verb + accomplishment

Coaching, Related, and/or Other Experience Category Guidelines

- Use the format under Teaching Experience Guidelines.
- Use the coaching experience category if the duty was contracted and the experience was significant. List minor coaching duties as bullet(s) under teaching experience.
- Use the related experience category if duties were related to teaching/administrative duties.
- Use the other experience category if the experience was significant, such as a former career, etc.

Professional Development Category Guidelines

- Cite the title first, then the organization, city, state, and date(s).
- There is no limit to the number of citations in this category.
- All training cited should be relevant to education and leadership.
- Note the hours spent if the number is significant.

Presentations and/or Publications Category Guidelines

- Cite all presentations and/or publications in APA style or another appropriate format.
- For five or fewer citations, use combinations of categories, such as presentations/publications. If there are more than five and at least two in each, use separate presentation and publication categories.
- Be sure to include all coauthors or copresenters.
- Consider citing dissertations, theses, and locally published curricular materials.

Professional Affiliations Category Guidelines

- Cite all current memberships in professional organizations.
- Note any offices held.
- Cite membership of significant duration in any professional organizations.
- Spell out complete names of organizations—do not use acronyms.

Honors/Awards/Scholarships Category Guidelines

- Use the relevant category if you have two or more citations—otherwise, list under teaching or administration.
- Use combinations of categories if appropriate.
- Cite honor, award, or scholarship, then the organization, city, state, and date.

Civic/Community Service Category Guidelines

- List title, organization, city, state, and date(s).
- Service cited should be related to goals or duties of the education profession, not purely personal.
- Service to a particular church or religion may be used; however, if it is simply personal information, it should not be cited.

References Category Guidelines

Use as last category on vita.

Including references with the vita is unethical, unless they were requested.

Be sure references gave permission to use their names.

References Page Guidelines

This *must* be a separate page. You must have a reference for each place you have worked. If you have more than six, limit to the last ten years. Use references from administrators—personal references are not appropriate. Cite references in order of priority—often only the first three are contacted.

- List name and title first.
- List name of school or organization next.
- List complete address, city, state, and ZIP code.
- List phone number with area code and e-mail address.
- Cite no more than six references.

Sample reference-page listing:

Dr. Bill Hickok, Principal
Page Elementary
184 Avenue C
Tombstone, AZ 85365
(520) 783-9999; bh@isp.edu

Frequently Asked Questions

Q: Shouldn't the vita be organized by years that appear in the left margin?

A: No. That is a style used for a business résumé, not an education vita.

Q: Should I use expensive paper with bright colors to make my vita stand out?

A: Neither expensive nor inexpensive paper is necessary, but you may use good quality paper. Brightly colored paper is a tactic used in the world of business; choose a neutral color Your experience and accomplishments should stand out, not the color of the paper.

Q: What should I do if my vita has time gaps?

A: You should exercise good judgment in this case. Often people with career gaps were raising children, tending to a sick family member, or using their time in a number of other reasonable ways. Others, however, were fired and could not get another job, were in drug rehabilitation, or have other, very personal reasons for career gaps. The point is that the reviewer of your vita may have doubts about which group you are in. Thus, unless your reasons are extremely personal, it is recommended that you provide some explanation for time gaps to allay the doubts of prospective employers.

Q: I do not have much in the leadership category. Should I list "leading students" in various activities or groups?

A: Your inexperience with leadership should motivate you to volunteer or apply for positions that will give you the necessary experience. Do not wait for an administrative position to gain leadership experience. There are many committees to chair, councils to serve on, and programs to lead while still teaching. Use your vita as a learning experience, and start filling in the gaps.

Q: How should I handle my coaching experience if it is quite extensive?

A: This is another judgment call. Much will depend on the position you are applying for. If, for example, you are applying for an assistant principal/athletic director position, then a complete listing of your coaching experience would be appropriate. If you are applying for solely an assistant principal position, limit your coaching experience category and use as much as appropriate in the leadership experience category. Many duties and responsibilities in athletics leadership are the same as those in school administration.

Q: I do not belong to any professional organizations. What should I do?

A: Join! Choose organizations appropriate to your career goals. High-school and middle-level principals may join the National Association of Secondary School Administrators (NASSP), elementary principals may join the National Association of Elementary Principals (NAESP), and those interested in curriculum development may join the Association for Supervision and Curriculum Development (ASCD). It is recommended that you also become active in the state affiliations for these professional organizations and read their journals regularly. Again, you do not have to wait to get the position to learn more about the position.

Q: I have not received any awards or honors. Do I need to compensate?

A: Many great educators never received any honors or awards. Others were honored or recognized after their careers ended. Honors and awards are bestowed by others—do not seek awards or honors but graciously accept them.

Q: Should I or shouldn't I list church activities?

A: Public education is bound by separation of church and state. Though active involvement with a particular church may denote many positive aspects of your service and character, some people may view it as interfering with the goals of public education. This is another judgment you must make.

Throughout your vita, letter of application, and interview, your responsibility is to clearly show the prospective school district who you are. This is your half of the work leading up to the contract. If a religious affiliation is such an important part of you that it goes with you into school, then it would be appropriate to cite your church work. If your religious affiliation is more personal in nature, then omitting it from your professional vita is appropriate.

Q: Why must the reference page be separate?

A: People willing to provide references for you assume districts very interested in hiring you will contact them. They should not have to provide information to every district where you applied. Therefore, it is considered unethical to provide references, unless requested in the job announcement or by the employer.

Q: Why should I list accomplishments?

A: Leaders accomplish things! This includes all education leaders, especially teachers. A vita that shows only where and when you worked does not give any indication of what you accomplished. Did you simply show up every day, or did you set goals and reach them? Accomplishment-oriented vitae do a much better job of showing which candidates are leaders. You should spend time analyzing your accomplishments (often forgotten or taken for granted), and list them under the appropriate categories.

Q: Can I change my vita?

A: Although you cannot change the facts, you can add facts and/or present them differently. Candidates design their vitae to match the positions they seek. For example, a district may desire curricular experience for an advertised position. In this case, an applicant could include a curriculum experience category and place it higher up in the list of categories used. Another example is a district that wants primary experience. In this case, the intern adds student teaching to the vita (normally not included) because that was his or her only primary experience. In short, try to match your vita with the position.

Sample Letter of Application and Guidelines

Sara Teacher
555 Maple Avenue
Miami, FL 50001
(999) 555-2122

April 15, 2012

Jack Armstrong, Personnel Director
ABC School District
Fort Lauderdale, FL 50000

This letter is to officially apply for the position of assistant principal at Baywatch Elementary School. I am fully aware of the duties and responsibilities of the position. My education, teaching experience, and certification meet all the posted requirements. After serious consideration, colleague support, and our administration's advice that I apply, I am certain that I am ready and prepared to assume the duties of the assistant principal.

I bring to the position 12 years of successful teaching. This includes four years of working with poor and minority students, two years with gifted and talented students, and eight years with numerous inclusive special education students. My students have performed better than the district and state average on tests, and very few have needed administrative disciplinary assistance. I have formed excellent relationships with parents and members of the community. My successful teaching performance has allowed me to serve in many leadership capacities. I have served as grade-level chair, Site Council representative, textbook committee chair, and math curriculum chair, and I have sponsored numerous student organizations and school programs.

My administrative internship allowed me to gain experience in observing teachers, disciplining students, budgeting and purchasing, developing staff, and managing general office duties and responsibilities. I have taken an active part in special education reviews, expulsion hearings, hiring interviews, parent conferences, and opening and ending school-year procedures. I understand the duties and operations of pupil and staff personnel, federal programs, transportation, athletics, and the curriculum department. I fully understand the role of the assistant principal and how to fulfill the needs of the various departments listed above.

I believe strongly in collaboration. This includes both the principal and the administrative staff and the faculty and students. I believe better decisions are made through participation and effective communication. I believe a school's first priority is student learning, whether academic or social. I believe in modeling fairness, openness, and honesty and always acting in an ethical manner. I believe what teachers and school administrators do has a much greater impact on others than what we say. I believe in the goodness of everyone and that care and concern for others is the first step to reaching them and finding ways for them to achieve success.

I believe my knowledge, skill, and experience can greatly assist the ABC District in meeting its vision, mission, and goals. I know I will assist teachers in planning and implementing lessons, remediation, and effective evaluation techniques. I will provide the support and leadership that the teachers and staff expect and desire. I will treat them with the respect and professionalism that they deserve. I will continue to set high expectations for the faculty, the students, and myself. Although my main focus is on support, motivation, and preventative strategies, I am very firm with individuals who do not meet expectations. I will demand excellence but will make all efforts to coach and assist people to reach excellence.

I have thoroughly enjoyed teaching and look forward to offering my experience, dedication, and skills to the faculty of Baywatch Elementary. I look forward to learning from and working with the current principal and fellow administrators. I appreciate your review of my letter, application, vita, and supporting documents. I look forward to discussing my role as assistant principal with you further. If any additional information is needed, please advise.

Respectfully,

Sara Teacher

Guidelines for the Letter of Application

In drafting the letter, the intern must assess his or her knowledge, disposition, skill, and the match to the position and district. The letter of application is the first impression you make of your career plans and experiences and how you may benefit the district. It should bring out the highlights of your vita and your knowledge of the district and position. It is an opportunity to explain and expand your vita with a sample of your writing and information about your philosophy and vision and the ways these conform to the needs and expectations of the school/district. The letter of application should include the following four sections:

Section 1—Intent of Letter

The first paragraph must begin with the purpose or intent of the letter; for example, you are officially applying for a particular position. Next, you should include that you are aware of the duties and responsibilities of the position. (If you are not currently knowledgeable about the position, be sure to acquire this knowledge during your internship experience.) Then include a statement about whether you have all the qualifications. If you do not, you should either specify which qualifications you do not have or indicate how or when you will acquire them.

Some applicants include a bit of personal information in this section. You might say that you are excited about the possibility of assuming this position or that you have been preparing for this position. If you decide to add a personal statement, be sure that it is honest and relevant.

Section 2—Your Half of the Match

This section includes the highlights of the knowledge, skills, and experience you can offer to the school/district. This is what the school district will get from you. Your goal in writing this section should be to inform the school/district about what you can do for it in the future versus what you accomplished for someone else in the past. An example of this is to state that you bring two years of experience in administering a primary reading program, instead of stating that you ran the Distar Program for the XYZ District. Although this is a subtle distinction, keep in mind that districts are looking for someone to belong and work for them, not an outsider.

This section is an opportunity to summarize your vita. For example, you can include the highest degree attained, the total number of years in education, relevant training or experience, etc. You can also provide further explanation and/or additional information not included in your vita. Examples could include your background, the types of students you have worked with, evaluations, successes with particular students, or other relevant information.

This section should also include your principles, beliefs, philosophy, and vision. The intent here is to provide a deeper understanding of your character and your style. Again, your letter needs to be oriented to the future and relate to how you will use your strengths in your new position. You should take plenty of time and do a lot of thinking when you draft this section. Consider the key beliefs and the guiding principles you will rely on in your new leadership position.

Section 3—Your Match with the District

Ideally, this section shows how your knowledge, skills, and experience meet the current and future needs of the district. This will require that you become knowledgeable about the history, current issues, and future demands of the district. You will need to gather information about the school/district and the particular position you seek. You must analyze the needs of the district and the position in light of your experience and abilities. This is your opportunity to show that you are the right match.

Section 4—Thankful, Bold Conclusion

This section concludes your letter of application. It should offer a thank you for the time and effort the district took to review your application materials. It should also make a bold statement of your expectation of being hired or continuing in the hiring process. An example of this is to state that you look forward to the further discussion of your accepting this position. This is much more positive and bold than concluding with a hope of hearing from them. If you accurately assess yourself and the district and know that you will be successful in meeting the needs of the position, you deserve to be bold. As with the first paragraph of the letter of application, you may choose to add any other personal or relevant items to this section. Use your best judgment.

Application Letter Guidelines

- Keep your letter short: one to one-and-a-half pages.
- Write in short, clear paragraphs.
- Describe yourself, not your previous employer.
- Outline the realization of the district's goals, not your own.
- Show that you have done your homework (know the school/district and its needs).
- Checked and recheck grammar, spelling, style, intent.
- Be positive, and avoid anything negative (districts want positive leadership).
- Describe yourself clearly; that will help the district assess the match between you and the position.

Standard One

An education leader promotes the success of every student by facilitating the development, articulation, implementation, and stewardship of a vision of learning that is shared and supported by all stakeholders.

Functions:

    A. Collaboratively develop and implement a shared vision and mission.

    B. Collect and use data to identify goals, assess organizational effectiveness, and promote organizational learning.

    C. Create and implement plans to achieve goals.

    D. Promote continuous and sustainable improvement.

    E. Monitor and evaluate progress and revise plans.

Standard Two

An education leader promotes the success of every student by advocating, nurturing, and sustaining a school culture and instructional program conducive to student learning and staff professional growth.

Functions:

    A. Nurture and sustain a culture of collaboration, trust, learning, and high expectations.

    B. Create a comprehensive, rigorous, and coherent curricular program.

    C. Create a personalized and motivating learning environment for students.

    D. Supervise instruction.

    E. Develop assessment and accountability systems to monitor student progress.

    F. Develop the instructional and leadership capacity of staff.

    G. Maximize time spent on quality instruction.

    H. Promote the use of the most effective and appropriate technologies to support teaching and learning.

    I. Monitor and evaluate the impact of the instructional program.

*As adopted by the National Policy Board for Educational Administration (NPBEA) on December 12, 2007

Standard Three

An education leader promotes the success of every student by ensuring management of the organization, the operation, and resources for a safe, efficient, and effective learning environment.

Functions:
   A. Monitor and evaluate management and operational systems.
   B. Obtain, allocate, align, and efficiently utilize human, fiscal, and technological resources.
   C. Promote and protect the welfare and safety of students and staff.
   D. Develop the capacity for distributed leadership.
   E. Ensure that teacher and organizational time is focused to support quality instruction and student learning.

Standard Four

An education leader promotes the success of every student by collaborating with faculty and community members, responding to diverse community interests and needs, and mobilizing community resources.

Functions:
   A. Collect and analyze data and information pertinent to the educational environment.
   B. Promote understanding, appreciation, and use of the community's diverse cultural, social, and intellectual resources.
   C. Build and sustain positive relationships with families and caregivers.
   D. Build and sustain productive relationships with community partners.

Standard Five

An education leader promotes the success of every student by acting with integrity, fairness, and in an ethical manner.

Functions:
   A. Ensure a system of accountability for every student's academic and social success.
   B. Model principles of self-awareness, reflective practice, transparency, and ethical behavior.
   C. Safeguard the values of democracy, equity, and diversity.
   D. Consider and evaluate the potential moral and legal consequences of decision making.
   E. Promote social justice, and ensure that individual student needs inform all aspects of schooling.

Standard Six

An education leader promotes the success of every student by understanding, responding to, and influencing the political, social, economic, legal, and cultural context.

Functions:

A. Advocate for children, families, and caregivers.
B. Act to influence local, district, state, and national decisions affecting student learning.
C. Assess, analyze, and anticipate emerging trends and initiatives in order to adapt leadership strategies.

Source: The Council of Chief State School Officers, Washington, DC, 2008.

National Association of Secondary School Principals (NASSP) 21st Century Skills

Educational Leadership

Setting Instructional Direction

- Implementing strategies for improving teaching and learning including putting programs and improvement efforts into action
- Developing a vision and establishing clear goals
- Providing direction in achieving stated goals
- Encouraging others to contribute to goal achievement
- Securing commitment to a course of action from individuals and groups

Teamwork

- Seeking and encouraging involvement of team members
- Modeling and encouraging the behaviors that move the group to task completion
- Supporting group accomplishment

Sensitivity

- Perceiving the needs and concerns of others
- Dealing tactfully with others in emotionally stressful situations or in conflict
- Knowing what information to communicate and to whom
- Relating to people of varying ethnic, cultural, and religious backgrounds

Resolving Complex Problems

Judgment

- Reaching logical conclusions and making high-quality decisions based on available information
- Giving priority and caution to significant issues
- Seeking out relevant data, facts, and impressions
- Analyzing and interpreting complex information

Results Orientation

- Assuming responsibility
- Recognizing when a decision is required

+ Taking prompt action as issues emerge
+ Resolving short-term issues while balancing them against long-term objectives

Organizational Ability

+ Planning and scheduling one's own and the work of others so that resources are used appropriately
+ Scheduling flow of activities
+ Establishing procedures to monitor projects
+ Practicing time and task management
+ Knowing what to delegate and to whom

Communication

Oral Communication

+ Clearly communicating
+ Making oral presentations that are clear and easy to understand.

Written Communication

+ Expressing ideas clearly in writing
+ Demonstrating technical proficiency
+ Writing appropriately for different audiences

Developing Self and Others

Development of Others

+ Teaching, coaching, and helping others
+ Providing specific feedback based on observations and data ·

Understanding Own Strengths and Weaknesses

+ Understanding personal strengths and weaknesses
+ Taking responsibility for improvement by actively pursuing developmental activities
+ Striving for continuous learning

Source: Selecting and Developing the 21st Century Principal Skills Assessment, NASSP, 2000.

National Association of Elementary School Principals (NAESP) Standards

Standard One: Lead Student and Adult Learning

Effective principals lead schools in a way that places student and adult learning at the center.

Standard Two: Lead Diverse Communities

Effective principals set high expectations and standards for the academic, social, emotional, and physical development of all students.

Standard Three: Lead 21st Century Learning

Effective principals demand content and instruction that ensure student achievement of agreed-upon standards.

Standard Four: Lead Continuous Improvement

Effective principals create a culture of continuous learning for adults tied to student learning and other school goals.

Standard Five: Lead Using Knowledge and Data

Effective principals manage data and knowledge to inform decisions and measure progress of student, adult, and school performance.

Standard Six: Lead Parent, Family, and Community Engagement

Effective principals actively engage the community to create shared responsibility for student performance and development.

Source: *Leading Learning Communities: Standards for What Principals Should Know and Be Able to Do (2nd Ed.)*. NAESP: Alexandria, VA.

ISTE National Educational Technology Standards for Administrators (NETS•A), 2009

1. Visionary Leadership

Educational Administrators inspire and lead development and implementation of a shared vision for comprehensive integration of technology to promote excellence and support transformation throughout the organization. Educational Administrators

    a. inspire and facilitate among all stakeholders a shared vision of purposeful change that maximizes use of digital-age resources to meet and exceed learning goals, support effective instructional practice, and maximize performance of district and school leaders

    b. engage in an ongoing process to develop, implement, and communicate technology-infused strategic plans aligned with a shared vision

    c. advocate on local, state and national levels for policies, programs, and funding to support implementation of a technology-infused vision and strategic plan

2. Digital Age Learning Culture

Educational Administrators create, promote, and sustain a dynamic, digital-age learning culture that provides a rigorous, relevant, and engaging education for all students. Educational Administrators

    a. ensure instructional innovation focused on continuous improvement of digital-age learning

    b. model and promote the frequent and effective use of technology for learning

    c. provide learner-centered environments equipped with technology and learning resources to meet the individual, diverse needs of all learners

    d. ensure effective practice in the study of technology and its infusion across the curriculum

    e. promote and participate in local, national, and global learning communities that stimulate innovation, creativity, and digital-age collaboration

3. Excellence in Professional Practice

Educational Administrators promote an environment of professional learning and innovation that empowers educators to enhance student learning through the infusion of contemporary technologies and digital resources. Educational Administrators

a. allocate time, resources, and access to ensure ongoing professional growth in technology fluency and integration
b. facilitate and participate in learning communities that stimulate, nurture, and support administrators, faculty, and staff in the study and use of technology
c. promote and model effective communication and collaboration among stakeholders using digital-age tools
d. stay abreast of educational research and emerging trends regarding effective use of technology, and encourage evaluation of new technologies for their potential to improve student learning

4. Systemic Improvement

Educational Administrators provide digital-age leadership and management to continuously improve the organization through the effective use of information and technology resources. Educational Administrators

a. lead purposeful change to maximize the achievement of learning goals through the appropriate use of technology and media-rich resources
b. collaborate to establish metrics, collect and analyze data, interpret results, and share findings to improve staff performance and student learning
c. recruit and retain highly competent personnel who use technology creatively and proficiently to advance academic and operational goals
d. establish and leverage strategic partnerships to support systemic improvement
e. establish and maintain a robust infrastructure for technology, including integrated, interoperable technology systems to support management, operations, teaching, and learning

5. Digital Citizenship

Educational Administrators model and facilitate understanding of social, ethical, and legal issues and responsibilities related to an evolving digital culture. Educational Administrators

    a.   ensure equitable access to appropriate digital tools and resources to meet the needs of all learners

    b.   promote, model, and establish policies for safe, legal, and ethical use of digital information and technology

    c.   promote and model responsible social interactions related to the use of technology and information

    d.   model and facilitate the development of a shared cultural understanding and involvement in global issues through the use of contemporary communication and collaboration tools

References

Alderfer, C. (1972). *Existence, relatedness, and growth.* New York, NY: Free Press.

American Association of School Administrators. (1960). *Professional administrators for America's schools (38th AASA Yearbook).* Washington, DC: National Educational Administration.

American Association of School Administrators. (1983). *Guidelines for the preparation of school administrators.* Arlington, VA: Author.

Ames, C. (1992). Classrooms: Goals, structures, and student motivation. *Journal of Educational Psychology, 84*(3), 261–271.

Angelo, R. W. Gestalt shift: In *Wittgenstein's logic of language.* Retrieved from www.roangelo.net/logwitt/gestalt-shift.html.

Bandura, A. (1986). *Social foundations of thought and action: A social cognitive theory.* Upper Saddle River, NJ: Prentice Hall.

Barnard, C. I. (1938). *The functions of the executive.* Cambridge, MA: Harvard University Press.

Barth, R. S. (1990). *Improving schools from within: Teachers, parents, and principals can make the difference.* San Francisco, CA: Jossey-Bass.

Bennis, W. B. (2000). *Managing the dream: Reflections on leadership and change.* Cambridge, MA: Perseus Publishing.

Bennis, W. B. (1989). *On becoming a leader.* Reading, MA: Addison-Wesley.

Bennis, W., & Nanus, B. (1985). *Leaders: The strategies for taking charge.* New York, NY: Harper & Row.

Cameron, J., & Pierce, W. (1997). Rewards, interest and performance: An evaluation of experimental findings. *American Compensation Association Journal, 6*(4), 9–31.

Carnegie, D. (1993). *The leader in you: How to win friends, influence people, and succeed in a changing world.* New York, NY: Simon & Schuster.

Cohen, M. D., March, J. D. and Olsen, J. P. (1972). A garbage can model of organizational choice. *Administrative Science Quarterly, 17*(1), 1–25.

Council of Chief State School Officers (2008). *National policy standards: ISLLC 2008.* Washington, DC: Author.

Covey, S. R. (2009). *The speed of trust: Live from L.A.* New York, NY: Covey.

Covey, S. R. (1989). *The seven habits of highly effective people.* New York, NY: Simon & Schuster.

Dewey, J. (1933). *How we think.* Amherst, NY: Prometheus Books.

Dewey, J. (1938). *Logic: The theory of inquiry.* New York: Holt, Rinehart, & Winston.

Dickmann, M. H., & Stanford-Blair, N. (2002). *Connecting leadership to the brain*. Thousand Oaks, CA: Corwin Press.

Dunn, R., & Dunn, K. (1977). *Administrator's guide to new programs for faculty management and evaluation*. Nyack, NY: Parker Publishing Company.

Erickson, D. A. (1981). A new strategy for school improvement. *Momentum, 12*(4), 46–48.

Etzioni, A. (1967). Mixed-scanning: A "third" approach to decision-making. *Public Administration Review, 27*(5), 385–392.

Evans, Robert. (1996). *The human side of school change*. San Francisco, CA: Jossey-Bass.

Festinger, L. (1957). *A theory of cognitive dissonance*. Evanston, IL: Row, Peterson and Company.

Forsyth, P. B. (1998). The school administrator supply: Summary of the national symposium. *Denver Symposium*. National Policy Board of Educational Administration.

French, J. R., & Raven, B. (1959). The bases for social power. In Darwin Cartwright (Ed.), *Studies in Social Power* (pp. 150–167). Ann Arbor: University of Michigan Press.

Fullan, M. (2001). *Leading in a culture of change*. New York, NY: John Wiley & Sons.

Fullan, M. (2001). *The new meaning of educational change* (3rd ed.). New York, NY: Teachers College Press.

Gardner, J. W. (1990). *On leadership*. New York, NY: Free Press.

Getzels, J. W. (1968). Administration as a social process. New York: Harper & Row.

Glasser, W. (1985). *Control theory in the classroom*. New York: Harper & Row.

Goleman, D. (2000). Leadership that gets results. *Harvard Business Review, March–April,* 78–90.

Goleman, D., Boyatzis, R., and McKee, A. (2002). *Primal leadership: Realizing the power of emotional intelligence*. Boston, MA: Harvard Business School Press.

Gorton, R. A., & Snowden, P. E. (2002). *School leadership and administration* (6th ed.). New York, NY: McGraw-Hill.

Green, A. (2011). *Beyond wealth*. Hoboken, NJ: John Wiley & Sons, Inc.

Greenberg, J., & Baron, R.A. (1997). *Behavior in organizations* (6th ed.). Englewood Cliffs, NJ: Prentice Hall.

Guarino, S. (1974). *Communications for supervisors*. Columbus, OH: Ohio Distributive Education Materials Lab.

Hall, G. E., & Hord, S. M. (2000), *Implementing change: Patterns, principles, and potholes*. Boston, MA: Allyn and Bacon.

Heintzman, M., Leathers, D. G., Parrot, R. L., & Cairns, A. B. (1993). Nonverbal rapport-building behaviors' effects on perception of a supervisor. *Management Communication Quarterly, 7*(2), 181–208.

Hendricks, G., & Ludeman, K. (1996). *The corporate mystic: A guidebook for visionaries with their feet on the ground*. New York, NY: Bantam Books.

Herzberg, F., Mausner, B., & Snyderman, B. (1959). *The motivation to work.* New York, NY: John Wiley & Sons, Inc.

Hoy, W. K., & Miskel, C. G. (2001). *Educational administration: Theory, research, and practice* (6th ed.). New York, NY: McGraw-Hill.

Hoyle, J. (1993). *Professional standards for the superintendency.* Arlington, VA: American Association of School Administrators.

Hoyle, J., English, F. W., & Steffy, B. E. (1990). *Skills for successful school leaders* (2nd ed.). Arlington, VA: American Association of School Administrators.

Hoyle, J., English, F. W., & Steffy, B. E. (1998). *Skills for successful 21st century school leaders.* Arlington, VA: American Association of School Administrators.

Jacobson, S. L. (1996). School leadership in an age of reform: New directions in principal preparation. *International Journal of Educational Reform, 5*(3), 271–277.

Johnson, L., Smith, R., Willis, H., Levine, A., & Haywood, K. (2011). *The 2011 horizon report.* Austin, TX: The New Media Consortium.

Kaplan, G. (1989). *Who runs our schools? The changing face of educational leadership.* Washington, DC: Institute for Educational Leadership.

Kerchner, C. (1993). The Strategy of Teaching Strategy. In P. Hallinger, K. Leithwood, and J. Murphy (Eds.), *Cognitive perspectives on educational leadership* (pp. 5–20). New York, NY: Teachers College Press.

Kohn, A. (1993). *Punished by rewards.* Boston, MA: Houghton Mifflin.

Kotter, J. P. (1998). What leaders really do. *Harvard Business Review on Leadership.* Boston, MA: Harvard Business School Press.

Leithwood, K., Louis, K. S., Anderson, S., & Wahlstrom, K. (2004). *How leadership influences student learning.* Wallace Foundation. Retrieved from http://mt.educarchile.cl/MT/jjbrunner/archives/libros/Leadership.pdf.

Lemke, C., Coughlin, E., Garcia, L., Reifsneider, D., & Baas, J. (2009). *Leadership for Web 2.0 in education: Promise and reality.* Culver City, CA: Meteri Group.

Lemke, C. & Coughlin, E. (2009). The change agents. *Educational Leadership, 67*(1), 54–59.

Levine, A. (2005). *Educating school leaders.* The Education Schools Project. Retrieved from www.edschools.org/pdf/Final313.pdf.

Lindblom, C. E. (1959). The science of "muddling through." *Public Administration Review, 19,* 79–88.

Lipham, J. M. (1964). Leadership and administration. In Daniel Griffiths (Ed.), *Behavioral sciences and educational administration. 63rd yearbook of the National Society for the Study of Education.* Chicago, IL: University of Chicago Press.

Maehr, M. L., & Midgley, C. (1991). Enhancing student motivation: A schoolwide approach. *Educational Psychologist, 26*(3/4), 399–427.

Marks, H. M., & Louis, K. S. (1997). Does teacher empowerment affect the classroom? The Implications of teacher empowerment for instructional practices and student academic performance. *Educational Evaluation and Policy Analysis, 19,* 245–275.

Martin, G. E. (1998). *Intern manual.* Flagstaff, AZ: Northern Arizona University.

Martin, G. E., Wright, W. F., Perry, E. A., & Amick, J. (2000). Reaching your goals for the internship: A university study. *Journal of the Intermountain Center for Education Effectiveness, 1*(1), 27–32.

Maslow, A. (1954). *Motivation and personality.* New York, NY: Harper & Brothers.

McClelland, D. (1961). *The achieving society.* New York, NY: Van Nostrand Reinhold.

Milstein, M. M., Bobroff, B. M., & Restine, L. N. (1991). *Internship programs in educational administration: A guide to preparing educational leaders.* New York, NY: Teachers College Press.

Mintzberg, H. (1989). *Mintzberg on management.* New York, NY: Free Press.

Murphy, J. (1992). *The landscape of leadership preparation: Reframing the education of school administrators.* Thousand Oaks, CA: Corwin Press, Inc.

Murphy, J., Shipman, N., and Pearlman, M. (1997). Strengthening educational leadership: The ISLLC standards, *Streamlined Seminar, 16,*(1), 1–4.

National Association of Elementary School Principals. (1990). *Principals for 21st century schools.* Alexandria, VA: Author.

National Association of Secondary School Principals. (1985). *Performance-based preparation of principals: A framework for improvement.* Reston, VA: Author.

National Council for Accreditation for Teacher Education. (1994). *NCATE refined standards.* Washington, DC: Author.

National Council for Accreditation for Teacher Education. (1982). *Standards for the accreditation of teacher education.* Washington, DC: Author.

National Policy Board for Educational Administration. (2002). *Advanced programs in educational leadership for principals, superintendents, curriculum directors, and supervisors.* Washington, DC: National Council for Accreditation for Teacher Education.

National Policy Board for Educational Administration. (1993). *Principals for our changing schools: Knowledge and skill base.* Fairfax, VA: Author.

National Council for Professors of Educational Administration. (2000). *Panel discussion with Joe Schneider, Neil Shipman, John Hoyle, and Chuck Achilles at the NCPEA Conference,* Ypsilanti, MI. Author.

National Research Council. Commission on Behavioral and Social Sciences and Education (2000). *How people learn: Brain, mind, experience, and school: Expanded edition.* Washington, DC: National Academies Press.

Prensky, M. (2001). Digital natives, digital immigrants. *On the Horizon.* Bradford, West Yorkshire, England: MCB University Press, *9*(5), 1–6.

Rice, E. M., & Schneider, G. T. (1994). A decade of teacher empowerment: An empirical analysis of teacher involvement in decision making, 1980–1991. *Journal of Educational Administration, 32*(1), 43–58.

Rinehart, J. S., Short, P. M., & Johnson, P. E. (1997). Empowerment and conflict at school-based and non-school-based sites in the United States. *Journal of International Studies in Educational Administration, 25,* 77–87.

Rinehart, J. S., Short, P. M., Short, R. J., & Eckley, M. (1998). Teacher empowerment and principal leadership: Understanding the influence process. *Educational Administration Quarterly, 34*(1), 630–649.

Rodgers, C. (2002). Defining reflection: Another look at John Dewey and reflective thinking. *Teachers College Record, 104*(4), 842–866.

Russell, T., & Munby, H. (1991). Reframing: The role of experience in developing teachers' professional knowledge. In D. Schön (Ed.), *The reflective turn: Case studies in and on educational practice* (pp. 164–187). New York, NY: Teachers College Press.

Schein, E. H. (1992). *Organizational culture and leadership.* San Francisco, CA: Jossey-Bass.

Schön, D., (Ed.), (1991). *The reflective turn: Case studies in and on educational practice.* New York, NY: Teachers College Press.

Senge, P., Kleiner, A., Roberts, C., Roth, G., Ross, R., & Smith, B. (1996). *The dance of change: The challenges of sustaining momentum in learning organizations.* New York, NY: Currency Doubleday.

Shibles, M. R. (1988). *School leadership preparation: A preface for action.* Washington, DC: American Association of Colleges for Teacher Education.

Simon, H. A. (1947). *Administrative behavior.* New York, NY: Macmillan.

Solomon, G., & Schrum, L. (2010). *Web 2.0: New tools, new schools.* Eugene, OR: International Society for Technology in Education.

Taylor, S., Rudolf, J., & Foldy, E. (2008). Teaching reflective practice in action science/action inquiry tradition: Key stages, concepts and practices. In P. Reason & H. Bradbury (Eds.), *The Sage handbook of action research: Participative inquiry and practice (2nd ed.)* (pp. 656–669). Thousand Oaks, CA: Sage.

Thomas, K. (1976). Conflict and conflict management. In M. D. Dunnette (Ed.), *Handbook of Industrial and Organizational Psychology* (pp. 889–936). Chicago, IL: Rand McNally.

University Council for Educational Administration. (1987). *Leaders for America's schools: The report of the National Commission on Excellence in Educational Administration.* Tempe, AZ: Author.

Vroom, V. (1964). *Work and motivation.* New York, NY: Wiley & Sons, Inc.

Vygotsky, L. S. (1978). *Mind in society: The development of higher psychological processes.* Cambridge, MA: Harvard University Press.

Web 2.0 In *Wikipedia.* Retrieved from http://en.wikipedia.org/wiki/Web_2.0

Weiner, B. (1986). *An attributional theory of motivation and emotion.* New York, NY: Springer-Verlag.

■ Index

A

Achievement Motivation Theory 90
Adult Learning 34, 45, 49, 153
Affiliative Style 94, 95
Alderfer, C. 89, 157
American Association of Colleges for Teacher Education xxii, 161
American Association of School Administrators xxii, xxv, 157, 159
Ames, C. 90, 157
Amick, J. xxiv, 160
Appendices xviii, xxiv
Assessments, School/District xi, xv, xx, xxv–xxvi, 23
Association for Supervision and Curriculum Development xxv, 137, 142
Attribution Theory 88–89

B

Bandura, A. 90, 157
Barnard, C. I. 82, 157
Baron, R. 97, 158
Barth, R. S. xxi, 157
Bennis, W. xxiii, 80, 91, 157
Bobroff, B. M. xxi, 160
Budget xvi, 18–19, 25, 49, 50, 57, 144

C

Cameron, J. 88, 157
Carnegie, D. 85, 157
Case—Sample 102–106
Change xvi, xvii, xxi–xxii, 34, 98–100, 157, 158, 159, 161
Classical model 82, 84
Climate xvi, xvii, xix, xxiv, 58, 61, 78, 98, 105–106, 110, 114, 117–119, 121, 122
Coaching Style 94–95
Co-curricular xvi, 34, 44, 54, 101
Cognitive Dissonance Theory 89, 158
Cohen, M. D. 83, 157
Collaboration xxii, 3, 7, 81, 82, 94, 103, 105, 125, 144, 148, 154–156
Collaborative Style 86
Communication xv, 19, 31, 79, 80, 84–86, 152, 158
Community/Business Involvement and Partnerships xvi, 58, 62
Community/Public Relations xvi, 58, 59
Conflict Resolution xvi, 68, 71, 80, 104
Consensus Building xvi, 27, 32
Council for Chief State School Officers xxiv, 150, 157
Covey, S. R. 79, 85, 157
Culture xvii, 97–100, 105, 117, 119, 154, 158, 161
Curriculum—Analysis of xvi, 35–36

D

Data Collection and Analysis xv, 27, 29, 30
Decision Making 4, 7, 81, 83–84, 103, 158
Developing Others xvii, 45, 78, 88
Dewey, J. 106, 157, 161
Dickmann, M. H. 127, 158
Directive Style 86, 94, 95, 105
Discipline xvi, 16, 18, 34, 44, 47, 54, 60
Diversity xvi, 4, 6, 7, 35, 58, 61, 97, 120, 149
Dunn, K. 93, 158
Dunn, R. 93, 158

E

Eckley, M. 97, 161
Educational Leadership Constituent Council vi, xxv
English, F. W. xxii, 91, 159
Enrichment Activities xvii, 109
Erickson, D. A. 98, 158
Ethics xvi, 7, 63, 65–67, 122, 123
Etzioni, A. 83, 158
Evaluation xv–xx, 12–14, 22, 43–45, 100–101, 105–106, 112–114, 129–134, 157, 158, 160
Evans, R. 100, 158
Expectancy Theory 89

F

Facility and Maintenance Administration xvi, 49, 53
Federal Programs xvi, 68, 70, 144
Festinger, L. 89, 158
Food Services xvi, 49, 55
Forsyth, P. B. xxi, 158
French, J. R. 95, 158
Fullan, M. 78, 98, 100, 158

G

Gardner, J. D. 80, 88, 158
Garbage Can model 82–84, 157
Getzels, J. W. 158
Glasser, W. 89, 158
Goal Theory of Motivation 90
Goleman, D. 94, 158
Gorton, R. A. 84, 158
Greenberg, J. 97, 158
Group Processes xvii, 78, 86, 91, 93, 104, 105
Guarino, S. 84, 158

H

Hall, G. E. 100, 158
Hallinger, K. 159
Heintzman, M. 85, 158
Hendricks, G. 100, 158
Herzberg, F. 89, 90, 159

Hierarchy of Human Needs 89
History of Education xvi, 63, 65
Hord, S. M. 100, 158
Hoy, W. K. 78, 81, 86, 159
Hoyle, J. xxii, 91, 159, 160

I
Incremental model 82–84
Instruction, supervision of, strategies xvi, 34, 38
Internship Report xviii, xxi, xxvi, 129, 132, 133
Interstate School Leaders Licensure Consortium
    (ISLLC) xxiv
Interpersonal Relationships xvi, 63, 67
Interviewing xvii, xxvi, 56, 77
ISLLC Dispositions xv, 5
ISLLC Educational Leadership Policy Standards 27,
    34, 49, 58, 63, 68, 148–150
Issue Resolution 87, 88

J
Jacobson, S. L. xxi, xxii, 159
Johnson, P. E. 97, 161
Journal v, xiii, xviii, xx, xxvi, 40, 46, 127, 128, 134, 142,
    157, 159, 160, 161

K
Kaplan, G. xxi, 159
Kohn, A. 88, 159
Kotter, J. P. 80, 159

L
Laissez-Faire Style 81, 82, 94, 95
Law xvi, 16, 17, 35, 44, 47, 52, 68, 69, 96, 113, 118, 122,
    124
Leadership Goals xv, xx, 23, 24, 133
Learning, 21st Century 153
Leithwood, K. xxiii, 159
Letter of Application xii, xviii, xxi, xxxvi, 132, 134,
    143–147
Lindblom, C. E. 83, 159
Lipham, J. M. 159
Log xx, xxvi, 29, 43, 128, 134
Louis, K. S. 97, 159
Ludeman, K. 100, 158

M
Maehr, M. L. 90, 159
Maintenance xvi, 49, 53, 54, 123
Management and Operations xvi, 7, 49, 51, 53, 55, 57,
    118
March, J. D. 83, 157
Marks, H. M. 97, 159
Martin, G. ii, v, x, xxiv, 160
Maslow, A. 89, 160
McClelland, D. 90, 160
Meetings 47, 67, 69, 86, 92, 93, 103–105, 123
Midgley, C. 90, 159
Milstein, M. M. xxi, 160
Mintzberg, H. 97, 160
Miskel, C. G. 78, 81, 86, 159
Mission xv, 28, 80-81, 100, 120, 148
Mixed Scanning model 82–84, 158

Monitoring xviii, 129
Motivation xvi, 23, 34, 40, 88–91, 104, 131, 145, 157,
    159–161
Motivation and Hygiene Theory 89
Murphy, J. xxiv, 159, 160
Muse, I. xxi

N
Nanus, B. 80, 157
NASSP Skills 27, 34, 49, 58, 63, 68
National Association of Elementary School Principals
    vi, xxii, xxv, 97, 153, 160
National Association of Secondary School Principals
    xxii, xxv, 137, 151, 152, 160
National Commission on Excellence in Educational
    Administration xxii, 161
National Council for Accreditation for Teacher Edu-
    cation xxii, 160
National Council for Professors of Educational
    Administration xxii, 160
National Policy Board for Educational Administra-
    tion v, vi, xxii, xxiv, xxv, 148, 158, 160
Networking xvii, xx, 25, 76, 125, 134
Notebook xvii, xx, 28-76, 110–124, 134

O
Office Administration xvi, 49, 50
Olsen, J. P. 83, 157

P
Parent Involvement xvi, xvii, 58, 60, 97, 120–121
Participative Style 94–95, 161
Pearlman, M. xxiv, 160
Perry, E. A. xxiv, 160
Personnel xvi, xvii, 49, 50, 54, 56, 100–101, 116, 118
Philosophy of Education xvi, 63, 65, 110, 146
Pierce, W. 88, 157
Plan Report xvii, 23, 76
Portfolio xviii, 132–134
Position Goals xvi, xxvi, 23, 63, 64
Power xvii, 78, 80, 89–91, 95–97, 105, 110, 120, 158
Professional Affiliations xvi, 68, 73, 137, 138, 140
Professional Development Plan xviii, 133–134
Professional Library xvi, 68, 74

Q, R
Raven, B. 95, 158
References xviii, 141, 143, 157
Reflective Practice xii, xvii, 4, 106–108, 161
Restine, L. N. xxi, 160
Rice, M. E. 97, 160
Rinehart, J. S. 97, 157, 161

S
Safety and Security 49
Satisficing model 82–84, 103, 104
Scheduling xvi, 34, 37, 152
Schein, E. H. 97, 161
Schneider, G. T. 97, 160
School Board xvi, 65, 68–69, 121
School Improvement Results xviii, 132
School Policies 118

Senge, P. 100, 161
Service xvi, xvii, 7–8, 24–76, 124, 141, 143
Shipman, N. xxiv, 160
Short, P. M. 97, 161
Short, R. J. 97, 161
Simon, H. A. 83, 161
Social Cognition Theory 90
Snowden, P. E. 84, 158
Staff Development xvi, 14, 34, 45, 97
Stanford-Blair, N. 127, 158
Steffy, B. E. xxii, 91, 159
Strategic Planning 112
Style, Leadership xvii, 32, 86–87, 93–97, 105
Student Services xvi, 34, 48

T
Taggart, G. L. 127
Technology xiv, xvi–xix, 19, 34, 41–42, 50, 124–127,
    154–156, 161
Technology Standards for School Administrators 50
Testing xvi, xvii, 34, 43, 101, 111, 114–116

Thomas, G. J. xxi
Thomas, K. 86, 161
Transportation xvi, 49, 54, 101

U
University Council for Educational Administration
    xxii, 161

V
Vignettes—See Enrichment activities
Vision xvi, xvii, xix, 2, 6, 27–33, 78, 80–81, 97, 103,
    110–112, 146, 148, 154, 158
Vita xii, xv, xviii, xx–xxii, xxv, xxvi, 1, 24, 132–146
Vroom, V. 89, 161

W, X, Y, Z
Wagner, T. 100
Weiner, B. 88, 161
Wilson, A. P. 127
Wright, W. F. xxiv, 160